LOVE IS A DANGEROUS WORD

T0355897

LOVE IS A
DANGEROUS
WORD
SELECTED POEMS

BY

ESSEX HEMPHILL

Edited by
ROBERT F. REID-PHARR and **JOHN KEENE**

Foreword by
ROBERT F. REID-PHARR

Afterword by
JOHN KEENE

A New Directions Paperback Original

Copyright © 1985, 1986, 1992 by Essex Hamphill
Copyright © 2025 by the Estate of Essex Hemphill
Copyright © 2025 by Robert F. Reid-Pharr
Copyright © 2025 by John Keene
Copyright © 2025 by New Directions Publishing Corporation

All rights reserved.
Except for brief passages quoted in a newspaper, magazine, radio, television, or website review, no part of this book may be reproduced in any form or by any means, electronic or mechanical, including photocopying and recording, or by any information storage and retrieval system, or be used to train generative artificial intelligence (AI) technologies or develop machine-learning language models, without permission in writing from the Publisher.

The Publisher gives special thanks to Brittany Dennison, who first encouraged New Directions to consider the work of Essex Hemphill.

Manufactured in the United States of America
First published as New Directions Paperbook 1625 in 2025
Book design by Marian Bantjes

Library of Congress Cataloging-in-Publication Data
Names: Hemphill, Essex, author. | Reid-Pharr, Robert, 1965– editor, writer of introduction. | Keene, John, 1965– writer of afterword.
Title: Love is a dangerous word : selected poems / by Essex Hemphill ; edited with an introduction by Robert F Reid-Pharr ; and an afterword by John Keene.
Description: First edition. | New York : New Directions Publishing, 2025.
Identifiers: LCCN 2024048661 | ISBN 9780811232340 (paperback)
Subjects: LCGFT: Poetry.
Classification: LCC PS3558.E47925 L68 2025 |
DDC 811/.54—dc23/eng/20241023
LC record available at https://lccn.loc.gov/2024048661

10 9 8 7 6 5 4 3 2 1

New Directions Books are published for James Laughlin
by New Directions Publishing Corporation
80 Eighth Avenue, New York 10011

CONTENTS

FOREWORD by Robert F. Reid-Pharr

> "My blessing is this. I do not stand alone bewildered and
> scared."[1]
> *Essex Hemphill*

It is unnerving to meet a genius. Stumbling into rooms filled with
smoke and sin, slouching in empty corners, breathing in the lux-
ury of gray freedom, and asking for nothing more exotic than
comfortable invisibility, one finds it clumsy and disquieting when
unexpectedly something opens, when a light is unsealed in the va-
cant dark and all eyes turn in its direction.

I met the poet, essayist, performance artist, and activist
Essex Hemphill in the fall of 1985. I was a junior at the University of
North Carolina doing a semester-long internship at two Washington,
D.C.–based lesbian and gay rights organizations, the Gay Rights
National Lobby and the National Coalition of Black Gays (later the
National Coalition of Black Lesbians and Gays), where most of my
time was spent helping to organize NCBG's upcoming convention
in Saint Louis, Missouri. The event was a remarkable and indeed
historic undertaking as it was a first of its kind, a large-scale gath-
ering of U.S.-based, Black LGBTQ activists, religious leaders, and
artists. The representation of writers and editors was particularly
striking. In addition to Hemphill, many of the founders of what
we now think of as the Black LGBTQ literary tradition—Barbara
Smith, Cheryl Clark, Jewel Gomez, Assotto Saint, Pat Parker, and
Joseph Beam—were in attendance. I was equal parts astonished and
thrilled. Essex's light was singular, his tone magnificent. I would soon
come to love hearing him present his work and took to memorizing
snatches of his poetry, pulling them out in moments of stress and
want, willing myself into a world broad and brave enough to hold
my desire. Still, from the very first moment that I met Essex, I knew
that though his talent was certainly unique, it was hardly singular.
His name was always mentioned in sentences crowded with proper
nouns. Though I often heard the words "Essex" and "genius" in the
same phrases, I just as often heard "Chris," "Michelle," "Wayson,"

---

1. See: "Black Nations/Queer Nations? Conference Video," CUNY Digital History
   Archive, accessed February 27, 2023, https://cdha.cuny.edu/items/show/8342.

"Joe," "Pat," "Yves," "Jewel," "Cheryl," "Barbara," and "Gil." Speak of Essex and you speak of a crowd, an army of poets and fanatics, valiantly trying to throw their voices at least as far as the nearest star. I met Essex Hemphill as part of an ensemble of activists and artists cultivating new languages, adding to the blue harmony and rattling syncopation of the movement. Indeed, it is from that group that I learned to appreciate the necessity of archives, the need to chronicle the journeys of our many tribes.

Essex Hemphill was born on April 16, 1957, in Chicago, Illinois, the second of Mantalene and Warren Hemphill's five children. He eventually moved with his family to southeast Washington, D.C., where he began writing, before graduating from Ballou High School in 1975 and enrolling at the University of Maryland, College Park. Spending only a year at the university, Hemphill shared a dorm room with Wayson Jones, another Black gay man and an aspiring musician, who would later become one of the gifted young poet's most significant collaborators. After leaving the University of Maryland, the young writer spent time in California before eventually returning to D.C. and enrolling at the University of the District of Columbia.[2] In 1979, he helped found the *Nethula Journal of Contemporary Literature*, inviting the D.C.-based poet E. Ethelbert Miller to become one of the magazine's coeditors. His instincts in bringing the older and much better-established Miller on board were absolutely correct. In addition to being the director of Howard University's African American Studies Resource Center, Miller was particularly well-connected in the Washington, D.C. literary arts scene. Indeed, it was through Ethelbert Miller that Hemphill met another of his most significant artistic partners, the filmmaker Michelle Parkerson, after Miller arranged for the two of them to share the stage at the 1980 Ascension Poetry Reading Series at Howard University's Founders Library.[3] Though this was neither artist's first public performance of their poetry it was certainly one of their most prominent. That 1980 reading helped not only to place Essex Hemphill at the center of Washington, D.C. cultural life but also to show him how warmly audiences responded to

---

2. See Martin Duberman, *Hold Tight Gently: Michael Callen, Essex Hemphill, and the Battlefield of AIDS* (New York: The New Press, 2014), 26

3. See Duberman, 30

his performances, paving the way for Hemphill, Wayson Jones, and their friend Larry Duckett to form the spoken-word group Cinque in 1982. That same year Essex produced his first two chapbooks, *Diamonds Was in the Kitty* and *Some of the People We Love,* followed by a third, *Plums,* in 1983. He then went on to release the collections *Earth Life* in 1985 and *Conditions* in 1986.

Ever ambitious, Essex Hemphill not only self-published his work, but also sent pieces out to key literary and popular journals, including *Obsidian, Black Scholar, Callaloo,* and *Essence.* It was not until 1986, however, that he and his writing would gain national and international attention. In that year, the writer and editor Joseph Beam published his groundbreaking collection *In the Life: A Black Gay Anthology* with Boston-based Alyson Books. The collection was significant not only because it gathered works by established writers like the novelist Samuel R. Delany, alongside those of less well-known individuals like Melvin Dixon and Assotto Saint, but also—and much more importantly—because it gave proof that the many individual efforts of Black lesbian, gay, bisexual, and trans people to represent their experiences could, if taken together, be recognized as a burgeoning cultural movement along the lines of both the Harlem Renaissance and the flowering of black feminist literature and culture that had begun in the late 1960s and that has never stopped. The anthology also helped bring Essex Hemphill to the attention of the U.S.- and U.K.-based filmmakers Marlon Riggs and Isaac Julien, who would later feature the poet and his poetry in their own breakout 1989 documentaries *Tongues Untied* (Riggs) and *Looking for Langston* (Julien).

Even more important, however, is the fact that after Joseph Beam's death from AIDS in 1988, Hemphill worked assiduously to bring the visionary anthologist's dream of a second collection of Black, gay male writing to fruition. Accepting an invitation from Joe's still grieving parents, Dorothy and Sun Beam, to complete their son's work and come live in their Philadelphia home to save money and receive their good food and company in the bargain, Hemphill decamped from Washington, living with the Beams until the anthology was completed in 1991. The second collection, *Brother to Brother: New Writings by Black Gay Men,* was larger and even more successful than the first. It brought together some three dozen individuals, including the filmmakers Marlon Riggs and Isaac Julien; the art historian Kobena Mercer; the novelists Melvin Dixon and Cary Alan Johnson; the poet Adrian Stanford (whose 1977 collection *Black and Queer* may be the first explicitly gay Black poetry collection published in the English language); and John Keene (who would go on to win a 2022 National Book Award for his own poetry collection *Punks*). I also show up in the anthology, ever blushing and clumsy, with a short bibliography of works by Black, gay men.

In 1992, Hemphill published his most ambitious single-authored work to date, *Ceremonies: Prose and Poetry,* a collection that included both new writing and selections from his chapbooks *Earth Life* and *Conditions.* That book would go on to win the 1993 National Library Association's Gay, Lesbian, and Bisexual New Author award, while Hemphill would earn both a Pew Charitable Trust Fellowship in the Arts and a prestigious residency at Los Angeles's famed Getty Center. By at least the midnineties then, Hemphill had built a truly enviable career in which he achieved national and international respect and acclaim. The cruelly obvious irony was that at exactly this moment in his still quite young life, it became ever clearer that his health was deteriorating. While many people were aware that Essex was suffering from Acquired Immune Deficiency Syndrome, he did not write extensively about the matter until 1994 when he released the poem "Vital Signs." He followed this with a deeply moving speech about AIDS, love, Black masculinity, and LGBTQ identity at the March 9–12 "Black Nations/Queer Nations?: Lesbian and Gay Sexualities in the African Diaspora" conference sponsored by the Center for Lesbian and Gay Studies at the Graduate Center of the City University of New York.

Though "Black Nations/Queer Nations?" was largely organized by academics and hosted on the campus of a university, it nonetheless continued the tradition of Black LGBTQ political and cultural gatherings epitomized by the 1985 National Coalition of Black Gays Conference where I first met Essex. Indeed, both Barbara Smith and Cheryl Clark, alums of the 1985 St. Louis conference, braved the snickering weather of late-winter New York to attend. Clark chaired the panel in which Essex gave his presentation. Alongside him were the novelist and critic Samuel Delany, the art historian Kobena Mercer, and the artist Coco Fusco, each of them extremely well-regarded intellectuals at the heights of their respective careers. Essex came last, beginning his comments by acknowledging his indebtedness to recently deceased pioneers of Black LGBTQ culture: Joseph Beam (1954–1988), Pat Parker (1944–1989), Audre Lorde (1934–1992), and Marlon Riggs (1957–1994). He then reminded his audience of the gritty truth that the line separating him from these only recently hallowed ancestors was becoming ever more thin. "One of the identities I presently wage, battle with, accept, reject, is being a person with AIDS," Essex said with a directness in no way dulled by his illness. He continued his speech in a manner that was equal parts vulnerable and defiant, stressing his desire to live as long and as well as he possibly could. He dedicated his comments to his new lover Roger and then announced, "If I had known sooner the true power of love to heal and affirm, I would have left the bathhouses, bushes, and bookstores immediately."

> I would have sooner done battle with my life-threatening addictions. I would have pursued a healthy way of living with more diligence than I gave to pursuing and busting a nut. Had I known sooner how simply beautiful love is, my self-destruction might have ended earlier.

It is best, I think, simply to acknowledge the hurt and the rage in these sentences. It is best to stand in the discomfort of hearing a remarkably talented poet, a month or so shy of his thirty-eighth birthday, tell us that he regretted significant portions of what was likely to be an already quite short life. He sat in front of an adoring audience, eyes damp, lips dry, and watched them watch him die. And yet even at this most tender of moments, Essex, ever fussy and meticulous, refused to succumb to melancholy. It wasn't not that he didn't understand how ugly and unfair his situation was. Instead, he simply continued to understand his life in its entirety—the bad and the good, the pathetic and the sublime. Even as he regretted his impending death, he also fully acknowledged the whole of what he had accomplished, reminding his listeners that though he sometimes suffered, he had also been "a brave, emboldened warrior preventing destruction from occurring."

In attempting to make sense of Essex Hemphill and his oeuvre, it is important to remember that there is genius and there is tradition, the one always shadowing the other, arriving too early or too late, cursing and giggling, preening in the commemoration of some occult knowledge, in which the distinctions between history, memory, beginning, end, justice, hope, fun, and failure lose meaning. Though it is impolite to say so, the entire history of African American writing and rhetoric is contradictory, multivoiced, and multivalenced. Phillis Wheatley, the mother of the grand tradition of African American poetry, was introduced to us in 1773 as the "Negro Servant to Mr. John Wheatley of Boston," and only then as the author of *Poems on Various Subjects, Religious and Moral*. The first words that we read written by Phillis herself are her dedication to her patron, the Right Honourable Countess of Huntingdon. This is followed by a preface in which Wheatley writes of her poems: "She had no intention ever to have published them; nor would they now have made their appearance but at the importunity of many of her best and most generous friends; to whom she considers herself as under the greatest obligations." This was followed by a brief letter from John Wheatley himself, explaining the details of the girl's life, particularly the miracle of his wife's purchasing the twelve-year-old unlikely genius fresh off the slaving ship *Phillis*, for which she was named. The book then gets down to business with a generous statement from eighteen prominent Massachusetts gentlemen, including Governor Hutchinson, Lieutenant Governor Oliver, and signer of the Declaration of Independence John Hancock, attesting to the veracity of the poems.

> We whose names are under-written, do assure the world that the poems specified in the following pages were (as we verily believe) written by Phillis, a young Negro Girl, who was but a few years since, brought an uncultivated barbarian from *Africa*, and has ever since been, and now is, under the disadvantage of serving as a slave in a family in this town. She has been examined by some of the best judges and is thought qualified to write them.

That is to say, the reader is subjected to pages and pages of apology before we get the first lines of Wheatley's verse: "Maecenas, you, beneath the myrtle shade/Read o'er what poets sung, and shepherds play'd." Indeed, Wheatley still had a bit of throat-clearing that she needed to do, penning an encomium to Gaius Clinius Maecenas, patron of the Augustan poets Horace and Virgil. Or to state the matter gracelessly, in order to enter the public sphere, Phillis had to figure out how to rid herself of her Barbarian rasp and pitch her voice in the dulcet tones perfected by unrepenting white supremacists.

The point here is that questions of authenticity and agency abound in African American literature. There are very few, if any, instances in which our culture can be said to have remained perfectly aloof from the ugliest aspects of Euro-American dominance and harassment. Ours is a tradition that gains its vibrancy precisely by continually negotiating wildly awkward positions within the cultures of the Americas and the larger world. This matter is made that much more vexing when we consider the many ways in which Black, gender, and sexual minorities have attempted to announce their existences and sensibilities within the bare-knuckle world of U.S. writing and publishing. Bruce Nugent's 1926 short story "Smoke, Lilies, and Jade," first published in the short-lived Harlem Renaissance journal *Fire*, is thought to be the first obvious example of explicitly homo*sexual* versus simply homoerotic literature by an African American. It follows the story of Alex, a Renaissance bohemian, who has a girlfriend, Melva, but who nonetheless cruises and brings home a Latino man whom he names Beauty.

> and Alex awoke ... Beauty's hair tickled his nose ... Beauty was smiling in his sleep ... half his face stained flush color by the sun ... the other half in shadow ... his eyelashes casting cobwebby blue shadows on his cheek ... his lips were so beautiful ... quizzical ... Alex wondered why he always thought of that passage from Wilde's *Salome* ... when he looked at Beauty's lips ... I would kiss your lips ... he *would* like to kiss Beauty's lips ... Alex flushed warm ... with shame ... or was it shame ... he reached across Beauty for a cigarette ... Beauty's cheek felt cool to his arm ... his hair felt soft ... Alex lay smoking ... such a dream ... red calla lilies ... red calla lilies ... and ... what could it all mean ... did dreams have meanings ... .

The provocation of this passage is not so much that Alex would like to kiss Beauty, a man with tickling hair, eyelashes casting cobwebby shadows, quizzical lips, and a "flush-colored" face. On the contrary, pitched correctly, the story might career into either tragedy or farce, thereby assuring readers that as pretty and available as Beauty might be, he exists so far outside the limits of the acceptable (or even the possible) that he poses no particular threat to the everyday progress of our lives. What Nugent does in "Smoke, Lilies, and Jade," however, is make it nearly impossible for the reader to decide exactly what to think or where to focus. Basic rules of composition have been thrown by the wayside. Nugent begins his sentences in full stride, never stopping for a breath. Beauty becomes a thing made entirely of stains and shadow. The very shape of his lips seems to be asking some unanswerable question, one provisionally addressed through reference to a half-remembered dream of red calla lilies. Where Phillis Wheatley hailed her readers with incredible deference, Nugent is idiosyncratic and provocative, tearing at the necessarily conservative nature of African American public discourse.

I would ask for grace and humility from readers who might too easily dismiss the criticisms of African American intellectuals like the great W. E. B. DuBois, who, after reading the bestselling 1928 novel *Home to Harlem,* by Nugent's close associate, the Harlem Renaissance writer Claude McKay, quipped that "the work nauseates me, and after the dirtiest parts of its filth I feel distinctly like taking a bath." DuBois stoutly critiqued the efforts of younger artists like Nugent and McKay because he believed that the sort of awkward characterizations of African Americans produced by writers like them simply reiterated the idea of the centerless/boundaryless black (proto)subjectivity that white supremacists believed to be the reality of both the enslaved and their descendants. Indeed, for DuBois, the problem with experimental writers like McKay and Nugent was that they, in effect, continued the apologetic dependency, speaking with "the white man's tongue" that presumably demeaned the poetry of Phillis Wheatley.

Still, Nugent and his coconspirators at *Fire!*—Wallace Thurman, Zora Neale Hurston, Aaron Douglas, John P. Davis, Gwendolyn Bennett, Countee Cullen, and Langston Hughes, all creative giants in their own rights—were intent upon expressing an essentially modernist and antisegregationist aesthetic. They were keenly interested in craft. At the same time, they drew on a wide range of references, voraciously consuming art and literature from the United States and Europe, hoping to bend the insights and techniques that they found to the specific cultural concerns—and conceits—of African Americans. Moreover, Countee Cullen, Wallace Thurman, and Langston Hughes have all been at least nominally registered as

Black, gay forefathers, no matter how awkward that label may be.

Strangely, though the remarkable flowering of African American literature that took place between the publication of "Smoke, Lilies, and Jade" in 1926 and Essex Hemphill's sharing a stage with Michelle Parkerson on the campus of Howard University in 1980 is undeniable, it is also the case that as Essex began his career, there continued to be surprisingly few images of gay male sexuality or identity within the African American literary tradition. Wallace Thurman's 1932 *Infants of the Spring*, Chester Himes's 1937 *Cast the First Stone*, James Baldwin's 1956 *Giovanni's Room*, Iceberg Slim's 1969 *Mama Black Widow: A Story of the South's Black Underworld*, Samuel Delany's 1976 *Triton*, and Adrian Stanford's 1977 *Black and Queer* all reference sexual minorities and genderqueer individuals, but other examples of this type of work are rare. This was the arena that Essex entered as he dared to add his own voice to the mix. He understood that he was heir to a remarkable tradition of African American writing that produced and supported him, but for which he was nonetheless an awkward fit. In a sense then, what Essex was after in his poetry was an attempt to erase what he took to be an artificial division between African American tradition and experimentation, root, and aspiration.

The last time I saw Essex was in the summer of 1995, perhaps six months before his death. I knew that he was ill, knew that some type of hideous countdown had begun. But on that day, glowering sunshine had settled in, and the streets of West Philadelphia were full of bustle and disheveled charm. Essex looked remarkable. He had moved apartments since I had last seen him and he enjoyed showing me the new space, pointing out its comfort and simplicity, and bragging that he had polyurethaned the floors himself. We reminded each other again that we were both neat, "well-put-together" people, indeed that our art depended upon it. Essex said, "How are you going to call spirits if your house is not in order?" and I very readily agreed.

I learned something vital that day. When two friends meet, the one young, the other very young, to say their final goodbyes, they immediately understand just how thin their words are. And when one of them walks away from close hugs and broad smiles to find himself choked and panicked in the overbright street, his arms wrapped around himself like a child anticipating disaster, he knows that there is nothing that he can say to calm the springing panic that has taken hold of his person. When he asks himself in a pique of anxious despair, "Will I be next?" only to realize that soon enough the answer to that question will be "Yes," he comes to see with vicious clarity the most basic of realities. There is nothing magical about our traditions, nothing so durable and precious in our culture that it is destined to live forever. Great poets all eventually die. The only question is whether their poems die with them. The last sentence that Essex ever said to me was "Take care of your blessings." He said it often, regularly sending me on my way with the sound of those six bright syllables ringing in my ears. That day though, I heard something new. I heard something about survival, diligence, grit, and passion, as well as about well-maintained apartments, and grace under thick pressure. I also learned something important about tradition. It always proceeds by fits and starts. I cannot draw a direct line from Phillis Wheatley to Richard Nugent, Chester Himes, James Baldwin, Iceberg Slim, Samuel Delany, and Essex Hemphill. I can, however, draw a crooked one. Traditions only last to the extent that they can be broken, manipulated, massaged, and extended. Essex Hemphill found himself looking into the mirror of African American literary tradition to find a carnivalesque image of himself looking back. So he smashed the mirror and tried to build something new with the shards. He never completed that work, but all the pieces are here waiting for someone to pick them up and begin again. These are your blessings. Take care.

LOVE IS A DANGEROUS WORD

AMERICAN HERO

I have nothing to lose tonight.
All my men surround me, panting,
as I spin the ball above our heads
on my middle finger.
It's a shimmering club light
and I'm dancing, slick in my sweat.
Squinting, I aim at the hole
fifty feet away. I let the tension go.
Shoot for the net. Choke it.
I never hear the ball
slap the backboard. I slam it
through the net. The crowd goes wild
for our win. I scored
thirty-two points this game
and they love me for it.
Everyone hollering
is a friend tonight.
But there are towns,
certain neighborhoods
where I'd be hard pressed
to hear them cheer
if I move on the block.

HEAVY BREATHING

... and the Negro every day lower, more cowardly, more sterile, less profound, more spent beyond himself, more separate from himself, more cunning with himself, less straight to himself,

I accept, I accept it all ... —*Aimé Césaire*,
Return to My Native Land

At the end of heavy breathing,
very little of my focus intentional,
I cross against the light of Mecca.
I recall few instances of piety
and strict obedience.
Nationalism disillusioned me.
My reflections can be traced
to protest slogans
and enchanted graffiti.
My sentiments—whimsical—
the dreams of a young, yearning bride.
Yes, I possess a mouth such as hers:
red, petulant, brutally pouting;
or at times I'm insatiable—
the vampire in the garden, demented
by the blood of a succulent cock.
I prowl in scant sheaths of latex.
I harbor no shame.
I solicit no pity.
I celebrate my natural tendencies,
photosynthesis, erotic customs.
I allow myself to dream of roses
though I know
the bloody war continues.

I am only sure of this:
I continue to awaken
in a rumpled black suit.
Pockets bulging with tools
and ancestral fossils.

A crusty wool suit
with salt on its collar.
I continue to awaken
shell-shocked, wondering
where I come from
beyond mother's womb,
father's sperm.
My past may be lost
beyond the Carolinas
North and South.
I may not recognize
the authenticity
of my Negritude
so slowly I awaken.

Silence continues
dismantling chromosomes.
Tampering with genetic codes.
I am sure of this
as I witness Washington
change its eye color
from brown to blue;
what kind of mutants are we now?
Why is some destruction so beautiful?

Do you think I could walk pleasantly?
and well-suited toward annihilation?
with a scrotal sack full
of primordial loneliness
swinging between my legs
like solid bells?

I am eager to burn
this threadbare masculinity,
this perpetual black suit
I have outgrown.

At the end of heavy breathing,
at the beginning of grief and terror,
on the X2, the bus I call a slave ship.
The majority of its riders Black.
Pressed to journey to Northeast
into voodoo ghettos
festering on the knuckles
of the "Negro Dream."

The X2 is a risky ride.
A cargo of block boys, urban pirates,
the Colt 45 and gold-neck-chain crew
are all part of this voyage,
like me, rooted to something here.

The women usually sit
at the front.
The unfortunate ones
who must ride in the back
with the fellas
often endure foul remarks;
the fellas are quick to call them
out of name, as if all females
between eight and eighty
are simply pussies with legs.

The timid men, scattered among
the boat crew and crack boys,
the frightened men
pretend invisibility
or fake fraternity
with a wink or nod.
Or they look the other way.
They have a sister on another bus,
a mother on some other train
enduring this same treatment.

There is never any protest.
No peer restraint. No control.
No one hollered STOP!
for Mrs. Fuller,
a Black mother murdered
in an alley near home.
Her rectum viciously raped
with a pipe. Repeatedly
sodomized repeatedly
sodomized before a crowd
that did not holler STOP!
Some of those watching knew her.
Knew her children.
Knew she was a member of the block.
Every participant was Black.
Every witness was Black.
Some were female
and Black.

There was no white man nearby shouting
"BLACK MAN, SHOVE IT IN HER ASS
TAKE SOME CRACK! SHOVE IT IN HER ASS,
AND THE REST OF YOU WATCH!"

At the end of heavy breathing
the funerals of my brothers
force me to wear
this scratchy black suit.
I should be naked
seeding their graves.
    I go to the place
    where the good feelin' awaits me
    self-destruction in my hand,
kneeling over a fucking toilet,
splattering my insides
in a stinking, shit-stained bowl.

I reduce loneliness to cheap green rum,
spicy chicken, glittering vomit.
     I go to the place
       where danger awaits me,
cake-walking
a precarious curb
on a comer
where the absence of doo-wop
is frightening.
The evidence of war
and extinction surround me.
I wanted to stay warm
at the bar,
play to the mischief,
the danger beneath a mustache.
The drag queen's perfume
lingers in my sweater
long after she dances
out of the low-rent light,
the cheap shots and catcalls
that demean bravery.

And though the room
is a little cold and shabby,
the music grating,
the drinks a little weak,
we are here
witnessing the popular one
in every boy's town.
A diva by design.
Giving us silicone titties
and dramatic lip synch.
We're crotch to ass,
shoulder to shoulder,
buddy to buddy,
squeezed in sleaze.

We want her to work us.
We throw money
at her feet.
We want her to work us,
let us see
the naked ass of truth.
We whistle for it,
applaud, shout vulgarities.
We dance like beasts
near the edge of light,
choking drinks.
Clutching money.
And here I am,
    flying high
    without ever leaving the ground
three rums firing me up.
The floor swirling.
Music thumping at my temple.
    In the morning
    I'll be all right.
    I know I'm hooked on the boy
    who makes slaves out of men.

I'm an oversexed
well-hung
Black Queen
influenced
by phrases like
"the repetition
of beauty."

        And you want me to sing
        "We Shall Overcome?"
        Do you daddy daddy
        do you want me to coo
        for your approval?

Do you want me
to squeeze my lips together
and suck you in?
Will I be a "brother" then?

I'm an oversexed
well-hung
Black Queen
influenced
by phrases like
"I am the love that dare not
speak its name."

And you want me to sing
"We Shall Overcome"?
Do you daddy daddy
do you want me to coo
for your approval?
Do you want me
to open my hole
and pull you in?
Will I be "visible" then?

I'm an oversexed well-hung
Black Queen
influenced
by phrases like
"Silence = death."

Dearly Beloved,
my flesh like all flesh
will be served
at the feast of worms.
I am looking
for signs of God
as I sodomize my prayers.

I move in and out of love
and pursuits of liberty,
spoon-fed on hypocrisy.
I throw up gasoline
and rubber bullets,
an environmental reflex.
Shackled to shimmy and shame,
I jam the freeway
with my vertigo. I return
to the beginning, to the opening of time
and wounds. I dance
in the searchlight
of a police cruiser.
I know I don't live *here* anymore
to witness.

I have been in the bathroom weeping
as silently as I could.
I don't want to alarm
the other young men.
It wasn't always this way.
I used to grin.
I used to dance.
The streets weren't always
sick with blood,
sick with drugs.
My life seems to be
marked down
for quick removal
from the shelf.
When I fuck
the salt tastes sweet.

At the end of heavy breathing
for the price of the ticket
we pay dearly, don't we darling?

Searching for evidence
of things not seen.
I am looking
for Giovanni's room
in this bathhouse.
I know he's here.

I cruise a black maze,
my white sail blowing full.
I wind my way through corridors
lined with identical doors
left ajar, slammed shut,
or thrown open to the dark.
Some rooms are lit and empty,
their previous tenant
soon-to-be-wiped-away,
then another will arrive
with towels and sheets.

We buy time here
so we can fuck each other.
Everyone hasn't gone to the moon.
Some of us are still here,
breathing heavy,
navigating this deadly
sexual turbulence;
perhaps we are
the unlucky ones.

Occasionally I long
for a dead man
I never slept with.
I saw you one night
in a dark room
caught in the bounce of light
from the corridor.

You were intent
on throwing dick
into the depths
of a squirming man
bent to the floor,
blood rushing
to both your heads.

I wanted to give you
my sweet man pussy,
but you grunted me away
and all other Black men
who tried to be near you.
Our beautiful nigga lips and limbs
stirred no desire in you.
Instead you chose blonde,
milk-toned creatures to bed.
But you were still one of us,
dark like us, despised like us.

Occasionally I long
to fuck a dead man
I never slept with.
I pump up my temperature
imagining his touch
as I stroke my wishbone,
wanting to raise him up alive,
wanting my fallen seed
to produce him full-grown
and breathing heavy
when it shoots
across my chest;
wanting him upon me,
alive and aggressive,
intent on his sweet buggery

even if my eyes do
lack a trace of blue

At the end of heavy breathing
the fire quickly diminishes.
Proof dries on my stomach.
I open my eyes, regret
I returned without my companion,
who moments ago held my nipple
bitten between his teeth,
as I thrashed about
on the mercy of his hand
whimpering in tongues.

At the end of heavy breathing
does it come to this?
Filtering language of necessity?
Stripping it of honesty?
Burning it with fissures
that have nothing to do with God?
The absolute evidence of place.
A common roof, discarded
rubbers, umbrellas,
the scratchy disc of memory.
The fatal glass slipper.
The sublimations
that make our erections falter.

At the end of heavy breathing
who will be responsible
for the destruction of human love?
Who are the heartless
sons of bitches
sucking blood from dreams
as they are born?

Who has the guts
to come forward
and testify?
Who will save
our sweet world?

We were promised
this would be a nigga fantasy
on the scale of Oz.
Instead we're humiliated,
disenchanted, suspicious.
I ask the scandal-infested leadership
"What is your malfunction? Tell us
how your automatic weapons
differ from the rest."

They respond with hand jive,
hoodoo hollering,
excuses to powder the nose,
or they simply disappear
like large sums of money.

And you want me to give you
a mandatory vote
because we are both Black
and descendants of oppression?
What will I get in return?
Hush money from the recreation fund?
A kilo of cocaine?
A boy for my bed
and a bimbo for my arm?
A tax break on my new home
west of the ghetto?

You promised
this would be a nigga fantasy

on the scale of Oz.
Instead, it's "Birth of a Nation"
and the only difference
is the white men
are played in Blackface.

At the end of heavy breathing
as the pickaninny frenzy escalates,
the home crew is illin'
on freak drugs
and afflicted racial pride.
The toll beyond counting,
the shimmering carcasses
all smell the same.
No matter which way
the wind blows
I lose a god
or a friend.

My grieving is too common
to arouse the glance of angels.
My shame is too easy to pick up
like a freak from the park
and go.

Urged to honor paranoia,
trained to trust a dream,
a reverend, hocus-pocus
handshakes; I risk becoming schizoid
shuffling between Black English
and assimilation.
My dreamscape is littered
with effigies of my heroes.
I journey across
my field of vision
raiding the tundra

of my imagination.
Three African rooftops
are aflame in my hand.
Compelled by desperation,
I plunder every bit of love
in my possession.
I am looking for an answer
to drugs and corruption.
I enter the diminishing
circumstance of prayer.
Inside a homemade Baptist church
perched on the edge
of the voodoo ghetto,
the murmurs of believers
rise and fall, exhaled
from a single spotted lung.
The congregation sings
to an out-of-tune piano
while death is rioting,
splashing blood about
like gasoline,
offering pieces of rock
in exchange
for throw-away dreams.

The lines of takers are too long.

Now is the time
to be an undertaker
in the ghetto,
a black dress seamstress.
Now is not the time
to be a Black mother
in the ghetto,
the father of sons,
the daughters of any of them.

At the end of heavy breathing
I engage in arguments
with my ancestral memories.
I'm not content
with nationalist propaganda.
I'm not content
loving my Black life
without question.
The answers of Negritude
are not absolute.
The dream of King
is incomplete.
I probe beneath skin surface.
I argue with my nappy hair,
my thick lips so difficult
to assimilate.
Up and down the block we battle,
cussing, kicking, screaming,
threatening to kill
with bare hands.

At the end of heavy breathing
the dream deferred
is in a museum
under glass and guard.
It costs five dollars
to see it on display.
We spend the day
viewing artifacts,
breathing heavy
on the glass
to see—
the skeletal remains
of black panthers,
pictures of bushes,
canisters of tears.

VISITING HOURS

The government pays me
nine thousand dollars a year
to protect the East Wing.
So I haunt it.

Visiting hours are over.
The silent sentry is on duty.
An electric eye patrols the premises.
I'm just here
putting mouth on the place.

Modigliani whispers to Matisse.
Matisse whispers to Picasso.
I kiss the Rose in my pocket
and tip easy through this tomb of thieves.

I'm weighted down with keys,
flashlight, walkie-talkie, a gun.
I'm expected to die, if necessary,
protecting European artwork
that robbed color and movement
from my life.

I'm the ghost in the Capital.
I did Vietnam
I served, like a dumb waiter.
My head is rigged with land mines,
but I keep cool,
waiting on every other Friday,
kissing the Rose,
catching some trim

I'm not protecting any more Europeans
with my life
I'll give this shit in here away
before I die for it.

Fuck a Remb-randt!

And if I ever go off,
you'd better look out, Mona Lisa.
I'll run through this gallery
with a can of red enamel paint
and spray everything in sight
like a cat in heat.

CIVIL SERVANT

for Nurse Eunice Rivers

I could perform my job no other way:
obey instructions or be dismissed,
which would end my nursing career.
I was a Colored nurse,
special, one of few.
I didn't question the authority
the government doctors exercised over me.
Their control of life and death
and my sense of duty and responsibility
were parallel and reciprocating.
My father, Tuskegee Institute, and Dr. Dibble
had trained me to obey
the instructions of white men
and all men.
I didn't talk back,
raise my voice in protest,
or demand the doctors save the men.
It wasn't my place to diagnose,
prescribe, or agitate.

When the doctors told me
to prevent the men
from getting treatment elsewhere
I did. I supplied their names
to all county health officials.
They agreed to withhold treatment
even after penicillin was discovered
to be an effective cure for bad blood.

The government doctors
viewed the men
as syphilis experiments.
I troubled myself
to remember their names.
I visited their homes
between annual checkups

to listen to their hearts
and feel their pulses.
They had aches and pains
and complaints too numerous to name,
but I soothed them. I tried.
I gave them spring tonic
for their blood.
I couldn't give them medicine.
I tried to care for everyone
including the women,
the old folks, and children.
I became an adopted member
of many of the families I visited.
I ate at their tables,
sat at their sickbeds,
mourned at their funerals.
I married one of their sons.

I never thought my duty
damned the men.
They were sick with bad blood,
but I thought they were lucky.
Most Colored folks in Macon
went from cradle to grave
without ever visiting a doctor.
The ones with bad blood were envied
because they received free
medical attention, food,
and rides to the health sites
come checkup time.

As the men died, I wept
with their wives and families.
I was there to comfort them,
to offer fifty dollars
if they let the doctors

"operate"—
cut open the deceased
from scrotum sack to skull.
They were usually horrified
by my offer,
fearing disfigurement
or the courting of blasphemy.
I assured them no one would know
that their hearts and brains
had been removed.
I suggested fifty dollars
could cover burial costs
and buy unexpected food
and clothes.

I never thought my silence
a symptom of bad blood.
I never considered my care complicity.
I was a Colored nurse, a proud
graduate of Tuskegee Institute,
one of few, honored by my profession.
I had orders, important duties,
a government career.

VOICES

In memory of William DeLoach, age five

My hands disappear
gloved in crimson flames.
They drip like wax
with your blood
burning the floor.
Nothing about this alarms me.
Nothing appears unusual.

I open the refrigerator
and place your head
on the top shelf.
Blood streaks
the white-shelled eggs below.
The voices of my waking world,
the captors of my sleep
are satisfied. Silent.
They are leaving
as I wax the kitchen floor
for the seventh time.

Over many months
the voices spoke to me.
As I tried to sleep,
when I rode the bus
or shopped for food
they were with me.
I tried to flee
but the voices pursued.
No drug soothed me.
No doctor could hear
what I heard.
The voices wanted me
to free my son
from his breed
and complexion.
"To dark to live!"

They implored.
I should have kept him
in my womb.
I don't hear his screams
when I close the refrigerator.

The evening the voices demanded,
"Deliver him—now!"
I withdrew the meat knife.
I called him to the kitchen
and beckoned him into my arms
to kiss me.
I slit his throat
as he tip-toed up
to put his lips to mine.
I licked his sweet blood
from my hands and blade.
I carved his heart from his chest
and hid it from a thief named God.

No, nothing about this alarmed me.
Nothing appeared unusual,
Your Honor.

FOR MY OWN PROTECTION

I want to start an organization
to save my life.
If whales, snails,
dogs, cats,
Chrysler, and Nixon
can be saved,
the lives of Black men
are priceless
and can be saved.
We should be able
to save each other.
I don't want to wait
for the Heritage Foundation
to release a study
stating Black men
are almost extinct.
I don't want to be
the living dead
pacified with drugs
and sex.

If a human chain
can be formed
around nuclear missile sites,
then surely Black men
can form human chains
around Anacostia, Harlem,
South Africa, Wall Street,
Hollywood, each other.

If we have to take tomorrow
with our blood are we ready?
Do our S curls,
dreadlocks, and Phillies
make us any more ready
than a bush or conkaline?

I'm not concerned
about the attire of a soldier.
All I want to know
for my own protection
is are we capable
of whatever
whenever?

WHEN MY BROTHER FELL
for Joseph Beam

When my brother fell
I picked up his weapons
and never once questioned
whether I could carry
the weight and grief,
the responsibility he shouldered.
I never questioned
whether I could aim
or be as precise as he.
He had fallen,
and the passing ceremonies
marking his death
did not stop the war.

Standing at the front lines
flanked by able brothers
who miss his eloquent courage,
his insistent voice
urging us to rebel,
urging us to not fear embracing
for more than sex,
for more than kisses
and notches in our belts.

Our loss is greater
than all the space
we fill with prayers
and praise.

He burned out
his pure life force
to bring us dignity,
to bring us a chance
to love ourselves
with commitment.

He knew the simple
spilling of seed
would not be enough
to bind us.

It is difficult
to stop marching, Joseph,
impossible to stop our assault.
The tributes and testimonies
in your honor
flare up like torches.
Every night
a light blazes for you
in one of our hearts.

There was no one lonelier
than you, Joseph.
Perhaps you wanted love
so desperately and pleaded
with God for the only mercy
that could be spared.
Perhaps God knew
you couldn't be given
more than public love
in this lifetime.

When I stand
on the front lines now,
cussing the lack of truth,
the absence of willful change
and strategic coalitions,
I realize sewing quilts
will not bring you back
nor save us.

It's too soon

to make monuments
for all we are losing,
for the lack of truth
as to why we are dying,
who wants us dead,
what purpose does it serve?

When my brother fell
I picked up his weapons.
I didn't question
whether I could aim
or be as precise as he.
A needle and thread
were not among
his things
I found.

FIXIN' THINGS
for Charles

I give you snatches of my boyhood
in exchange for pictures of yours.
Often you voice difficult memories
that I keep silent regarding home.

In retrospect, it wasn't the sound
of my mother crying that hurt most,
it was the sound of my father leaving
his marriage, his house, his familiars.

In the debris of ruptured bloodlines,
in the domestic violence of our families,
in the turbulence we call love was bred
the possibility of my dysfunction, and yours.

I tell you of the hatred
that seized the boyhoods
of my brother and me,
how we fought violently in public,

drawing blood as if it would
allow us to see
what was wrong with it,
with him, with me.

We are men now, he with a family;
I have a cat and a thousand poems.
We have accepted what we can of ourselves:
my homo life, his hyper masculinity, the same
        difference.

How does the world see my brother?
How is he treated, how is he approached?
What dreams does he keep from childhood?
What does he look like as a father?

I know little of this about him
as I rush from airports to hotels to podiums.
I know little of this as I go about
publicly advocating for Black brotherhood.

So when I am with you, my friend,
and we open our hearts to one another,
I wonder why I have never
done this with my blood brother?

You and I afford ourselves the space to release
the anguish; across a simple kitchen table
we examine scars, we teach ourselves to make
          power
and beauty of scars, a skill we learn with great
          effort.

Why I have never created such a space
for speaking to my brother, and how to now,
now as I move toward the middle years
losing more than I gain to live.

How to address this is the dream that eludes my
          blue nights.
O sweet dream, when will you come to me with
          answers?
Must I beg? Of the many issues that concern me,
how to speak to my brother is a mystery.

Is it a new language we must learn?
Is it a miracle sign that foretells of us
speaking in tongues and finally understanding?
These are the elusive questions that foil me.

Why are we unable to say this
to our blood brothers, share this with them,

across a common table touch, create
a trusted fellowship, why can't we?

Why is the world always easier to fix
than our own homes?

COMMITMENTS

I will always be there.
When the silence is exhumed.
When the photographs are examined
I will be pictured smiling
among siblings, parents,
nieces and nephews.

In the background of the photographs:
the hazy smoke of barbecue,
a checkered red and white tablecloth
laden with blackened chicken,
glistening ribs, paper plates,
bottles of beer and pop.

In the photos,
the smallest children
are always held by their parents.
My arms are always empty, or around
the shoulders of unsuspecting aunts
expecting to throw rice at me someday.

Or picture tinsel, candles,
ornamented imitation trees,
or another table, this one
set for Thanksgiving,
a turkey steaming the lens.

My arms are empty
in those photos, too,
so empty they would break
around a lover.

I am always there
for the critical emergencies,
graduations,
the middle of the night.

I am the invisible son.
In the family photographs
nothing appears out of character.
I smile as I serve my duty.

RIGHTS AND PERMISSIONS

Sometimes I hold
my warm seed
up to my mouth
very close
to my parched lips
and whisper
"I'm sorry,"
before I turn my hand
over the toilet
and listen to the seed
splash into the water.

I rinse what remains
down the drain,
dry my hands—
they return
to their tasks
as if nothing
out of place
has occurred.

I go on being,
wearing my shirts
and trousers,
voting, praying,
paying rent,
pissing in public,
cussing cabs,
fussing with utilities.

What I learn
as age advances,
relentless pillager,
is that we shrink
inside our shirts
and trousers,

or we spread
beyond the seams.
The hair we cherished
disappears.

Sometimes I hold
my warm seed
up to my mouth
and kiss it.

OBJECT LESSONS

If I am comfortable
on the pedestal
you are looking at,
if I am indolent and content
to lay here on my stomach,
my determinations
indulged and glistening
in baby oil and sweat,
if I want to be here, a pet,
to be touched, a toy,
if I choose
to be liked in this way,
if I desire to be object,
to be sexualized
in this object way,
by one or two at a time,
for a night or a thousand days,
for money or power,
for the awesome orgasms
to be had, to be coveted,
or for my own selfish wantonness,
for the feeling of being
pleasure, being touched.
The pedestal was here,
so I climbed up.
I located myself.
I appropriated this context.
It was my fantasy,
my desire to do so
and lie here
on my stomach.
Why are you looking?
What do you wanna
do about it?

INVITATIONS ALL AROUND

If he is your lover,
never mind.
Perhaps, if we ask
he will join us.

THE OCCUPIED TERRITORIES

You are not to touch yourself
in any way
or be familiar with ecstasy.
You are not to touch
anyone of your own sex
or outside of your race
then talk about it,
photograph it, write it down
in explicit details, or paint it
red, orange, blue, or dance
in honor of its power, dance
for its beauty, dance
because it's yours.

You are not to touch other flesh
without a police permit.
You have no privacy—
the State wants to seize your bed
and sleep with you.
The State wants to control
your sexuality, your birth rate,
your passion.
The message is clear:
your penis, your vagina,
your testicles, your womb,
your anus, your orgasm,
these belong to the State.
You are not to touch yourself
or be familiar with ecstasy.
The erogenous zones
are not demilitarized.

SONG FOR RAPUNZEL

His hair
almost touches
his shoulders.
He dreams
of long braids,
ladders,
vines of hair.
He stands
like Rapunzel,
waiting on his balcony
to be rescued
from the fire-breathing
dragons of loneliness.
They breathe
at his hips
and thighs
the years soften
as they turn.
How long must he dream
ladders no one climbs?
He stands like Rapunzel,
growing deaf,
waiting
for a call.

THE TOMB OF SORROW

for Wolf

> I cannot say
> that I have gone to hell
> for your love
> but often
> found myself there
> in your pursuit.
> > —*William Carlos Williams*
> > "Asphodel, That Greeny Flower"

I

Gunshots ring out above our heads
as we sit beneath your favorite tree,
in this park called Meridian Hill,
called Malcom X, that you call
the "Tomb of Sorrow, "
(and claim to be its gatekeeper);
in the cool air lingering after the rain,
the men return to the Wailing Wall
to throw laughter and sad glances
into the fountains below,
or they scream out
for a stud by any name,
their beautiful asses
rimmed by the moon.

Gunshots ring out above our heads
as we cock dance
beneath your favorite tree.
There are no invectives
to use against us.
We are exhausted
from dreaming wet dreams,
afraid of the passion
that briefly consoles us.
I ask no more of you
than I ask of myself:

no more guilt, no more pity.
Occult risks await us
at the edge of restraint.

These are meaningless kisses
(aren't they?)
that we pass back and forth
like poppers and crack pipes,
and for a fleeting moment,
in a flash of heat and consent,
we release our souls
to hover above our bodies;
we believe our shuddering orgasms
are transcendental;
our loneliness manifests itself
as seed we cannot take
or give.

Gunshots ring out above our heads,
a few of us are seeking romance,
others a piece of ass,
some—a stroke of dick.
The rest of us are killing.
The rest of us get killed.

II

When I die,
honey chil',
my angels
will be tall
Black drag queens.
I will eat their stockings
as they fling them
into the blue
shadows of dawn.

I will suck
their purple lips
to anoint my mouth
for the utterance of prayer.

My witnesses
will have to answer
to go-go music.
Dancing and sweat
will be required
at my funeral.

Someone will have to answer
the mail I leave,
the messages
on my phone service;
someone else
will have to tend
to the aching
that drove me
to seek soul.

Everything different
tests my faith.
I have stood in places
where the absence of light
allowed me to live longer,
while at the same time
it rendered me blind.

I struggle against
plagues, plots,
pressure,
paranoia.
Everyone wants a price
for living.

When I die,
my angels,
immaculate
Black diva
drag queens,
all of them
sequined
and seductive,
some of them
will come back
to haunt you,
I promise,
honey chil'.

III

You stood beneath a tree
guarding moonlight,
clothed in military fatigues,
black boots, shadows,
winter rain, midnight,
jerking your dick slowly,
deliberately calling attention
to its proud length
and swollen head.
A warrior dick,
a dick of consequences
nodded knowingly at me.

You were stirring it
when I approached,
making it swell more,
allowing raindrops escaping
through leaves and branches
to bounce off of it
and shatter like doubt.

Among the strangest gifts
I received from you
(and I returned them all)—
a chest of dark, ancient wood,
inside: red velvet cushions,
coins, paper money
from around the world.
A red book of hand-drawn runes,
a kufi, prayer beads,
a broken timepiece—
the stench of dry manure.

And there were other things
never to be forgotten—
a silver horse head
to hold my chain of keys,
a Christian sword,
black candles,
black dolls
with big dicks
and blue dreads
that you nailed
above my bed
to ensure fidelity.
A beer bottle filled
with hand-drawn soap,
a specificity—
a description of your life,
beliefs, present work,
weight and height;
declarations of love
which I accepted,
overlooking how I disguised
my real motivations—
a desire to keep

some dick at home
and love it as best I can.

I was on duty to your madness
like a night nurse
in a cancer ward.
Not one alarm went off
as I laid with you, Succubus.
I've dreamed of you
standing outside my soul
beneath a freakish tree,
stroking your dick
which is longer
in the dream, but I,
unable to be moved
and enchanted,
rebuke you.
I vomit up your snake
and hack it to pieces,
laughing as I strike.

No, I was not
your pussy,
she would be
your dead wife.
I believe you
dispatched her soul
or turned her into a cat.
I was your man lover,
gambling dangerously
with my soul.
I was determined to love you
but you were haunted
by Vietnam,
taunted by demons.

In my arms you dreamed
of tropical jungles,
young village girls
with razors embedded in their pussies,
lethal chopsticks
hidden in their hair,
their nipples clenched
like grenade pins
between your grinding teeth.
You rocked and kicked
in your troubled sleep,
as though you were fucking
one of those dangerous cunts,
and I was by your side,
unable to hex it away,
or accept that peace
means nothing to you,
and the dreams you suffer
may be my only revenge.

IV

It was an end to masturbation.
That's what I was seeking.
I couldn't say it then, no,
I couldn't say it then.

When you told me
your first lover,
a white man,
wanted you to spit,
shit, piss on,
fist-fuck and
throw him down stairs,
alarms should have
blared forth

like hordes
of screaming queens.

When you said
in the beginning
you beat up Black men
after you fucked them,
when you said
in the last year
you were buying crack
for Black men
who let you fuck 'em,
alarms should have
deafened me for life.

When you told me
you once tied a naked man
between two trees
in an isolated,
wooded area,
debased him,
leaving him there
for several days,
then sent others
to rape him and feed him,
my head should have exploded
into shrapnel
and killed us both.

When you swore you loved me
and claimed to be sent here
to protect me,
I should have put bullets
in my temple
or flaming swords
up my ass.

Feeling my usual
sexual vexations,
I came here then,
seeking only pleasure,
dressed for the easy seduction,
I never considered
carrying a cross.
I had no intention
of being another queen
looking out
at the morning rain
from the Wailing Wall,
hoping to spy a brutish man
with a nearby home.
Slouching through Homo Heights,
I came to the Tomb of Sorrow
seeking penetration and Black seed.
My self-inflicted injuries occurred
when I began loving you
and trusting you.

V

Where's my needle?
Fetch my thread.
I'm going to sew
a prince to my bed.

Stitch by stitch
I'll shuttle my thread
in and out
and around his head.

Over his fingers
down to his toes,

up his crotch,
through his nose.

Be he live
or be he dead
I'll sew his heart
to my bed.

Stitch by stitch
I shuttle my thread
in and out
and around his head.

VI

Through some other
set of eyes
I have to see you
block boy,
fantasy charmer,
object of my desire,
my scorn,
abuser of my affections,
curse and beauty,
tough/soft young men,
masked men,
cussing men,
sweet swaggering
buffalo soldiers.

Through some other
set of eyes
I must recognize
our positions
are often equal.

We are worth more
to each other
than twenty dollars,
bags of crack,
bullets piercing our skulls.
I can't hope to help
save us from destruction
by using my bed
as a pagan temple,
a false safe house.
There are other ways
to cross the nights,
to form lasting bonds;
there are other desires
as consuming as flesh.
There are ways
to respect our beauty.

Through some other set
of common eyes
I have to behold you
again, homeboy.
I rummage through
ancestral memories
in search of the
original tribes
that fathered us.
I want to remember
the exact practices
of civility
we agreed upon.
I want us to remember
the nobility of decency.

At the end of the day,
through some other vision,

perhaps the consequence
of growing firm and older,
I see the thorns of the rose
are not my enemy.
I strive to see this
in each of us—
O ancient petals,
O recent blooms.

SO MANY DREAMS

Had I been clear-headed
there would have been
no pattern of sanity
to follow.
Out of this confusion
I bring my heart,
a pale blue crystal,
a single rose,
a kiss long held for you
before the myth of Atlantis
was created to challenge
the genius of
Memphis and Senegal.
I long for the occult sciences
to inform you of my affections,
and if this evidence
is insufficient,
then let a single dream
containing the content of my soul
spill throughout your sleep,
and from all the nights
I have longed for you
in a spell of masturbation,
take whatever voice I would use
to call out your name
in the sleeping garden,
take whatever suits you,
my love, for now.

FAMILY JEWELS
for Washington, D.C.

I live in a town
where pretense and bone structure
prevail as credentials
of status and beauty—
a town bewitched
by mirrors, horoscopes,
and corruption.

I intrude on this nightmare,
arm outstretched from curbside.
I'm not pointing to Zimbabwe.
I want a cab
to take me to Southeast
so I can visit my mother.
I'm not ashamed to cross
the bridge that takes me there.

No matter where I live
or what I wear
the cabs speed by.
Or they suddenly brake a
few feet away
spewing fumes in my face
to serve a fair-skinned fare.

I live in a town
where everyone is afraid
of the dark.
I stand my ground unarmed
facing a mounting disrespect,
a diminishing patience,
a need for defense.

In passing headlights
I appear to be a criminal.
I'm a weird-looking

muthafucka.
Shaggy green hair sprouts all over me.
My shoulders hunch and bulge. I growl
as blood drips from my glinting fangs

My mother's flowers are wilting
while I wait.
Our dinner is cold
by now.

I live in a town
where pretense and structure
are devices of cruelty—
a town bewitched
by mirrors, horoscopes
and blood.

SOFT TARGETS

for Black Girls

He was arrested and detained
for nailing Barbie doll heads
to telephone poles.

He was beaten
while in custody, accused
of defacing public property.

After healing, he resumed
his irreverent campaign,
this outlawed spook terrorist
continued hammering horse nails

through Barbie heads,
and setting them aflame.

Barbie never told Black girls
they are beautiful.

She never acknowledged
their breathtaking Negritude.

She never told them
to possess their own souls.

They were merely shadows
clutching the edges of her mirror.

Barbie has never told Black girls
they are beautiful,

not in the ghetto evenings
after double dutch,

nor in the integrated suburbs
after ballet class.

CORDON NEGRO

I drink champagne early in the morning
instead of leaving my house
with an M16 and nowhere to go.

I die twice as fast
as any other American
between eighteen and thirty-five.
This disturbs me,
but I try not to show it in public.

Each morning I open my eyes is a miracle.
The blessing of opening them
is temporary on any given day.
I could be taken out,
I could go off,
I could forget to be careful.
Even my brothers, hunted, hunt me.
I'm the only one who values my life
and sometimes I don't give a damn.

My love life can kill me.
I'm faced daily with choosing violence
or a demeanor that saves every other life
but my own.

I won't cross over.
It's time someone came to me
not to patronize me physically,
sexually or humorously.

I'm sick of being an endangered species,
sick of being a goddamn statistic.
So what are my choices?

I could leave with no intention
of coming home tonight,

go crazy downtown and raise hell
on a rooftop with my rifle.
I could live for a brief moment
on the six o'clock news,
or masquerade another day
through the corridors of commerce
and American dreams.

I'm dying twice as fast
as any other American.
So I pour myself a glass of champagne,
I cut it with a drop of orange juice.

After I swallow my liquid Valium,
my private celebration
for being alive this morning,
I leave my shelter,
I guard my life with no apologies.
My concerns are small
and personal.

BLACK MACHISMO

Metaphorically speaking
his black dick is so big
when it stands up erect
it silences
the sound of his voice.
It obscures his view
of the territory, his history,
the cosmology of his identity
is rendered invisible.

When his big black dick
is not erect
it drags behind him,
a heavy, obtuse thing,
his balls and chains
clattering, making
so much noise
I cannot hear him
even if I want to listen.

TO SOME SUPPOSED BROTHERS

You judge a woman
by the length of her skirt,
by the way she walks,
talks, looks, and acts;
by the color of her skin you judge,
and will call her "Bitch!"
"Black bitch!"
if she doesn't answer to your:
"Hey baby, whatcha gonna say
to a man."

You judge a woman
by the job she holds,
the number of children she's had,
the number of digits on her check,
by the many men she may have laid with
and wonder what jive murphy
you'll run on her this time.

You tell a woman
every poetic love line
you can think of,
then like the desperate needle
of a strung-out junkie
you plunge into her veins,
travel wildly through her blood,
confuse her mind, make her hate,
and be cold to the men to come,
destroying the thread of calm
she held.

You judge a woman
by what she can do for you alone
but there's no need
for slaves to have slaves.

You judge a woman
by impressions you think you've made.
Ask and she gives,
take without asking,
beat on her and she'll obey,
throw her name up and down the streets
like some loose whistle—
knowing her neighbors will talk.
Her friends will chew her name,
Her family's blood will run loose
like a broken creek.
And when you're gone,
a woman is left
healing her wounds alone.

But we so-called men,
we so-called brothers,
wonder why it's so hard
to love our women
when we're about loving them
the way America
loves us.

GARDENIAS

Another station, a new town.
The same COLORED and
WHITE ONLY signs.
By now I shouldn't really care
but it amazes me still.

Every town since St. Louis
has been mean and nasty.
Signs everywhere,
and in some places
whorehouses
for COLORED ONLY
but no proper places
where a lady can pee.

Tonight, once again
I tie my hair up
with gardenias.
I blacken my face
and set myself afire
singing for my man.

Where O where
can he be, can he be?
Out looking for a place
without signs,
somewhere better
than New York
to hang his hat
or to just watch me
unbraid gardenias
from my hair.

I WANT TO TALK ABOUT YOU

Wizards. All of them. Wizards.
Gravel in their throats.
Worrying the line.
Horn to bleeding lips.
Fingers thrashing white keys
cascading black.
Wizards of impulse and verve,
blizzard blowing wizards blowing
blue-red-bright-black-blow-ing
a capella saxophones.
Scat wizards trans-
muting anguish
into bird songs.

Soul boys who found freedom
in the pedals and sticks
of their instruments,
who took freedom,
putting out in jook joints
and dance halls,
putting up on
chicken-bone-buses
'cross country
that kept on going
through cracker towns,
'cause there was no place
for a busload
of Colored musicians
to stop.

This was before Martin dreamed,
before panthers stalked,
before fire spoke eloquently
like our trumpeters.

Gardenias, trains, cannonballs—

anything we needed
they became.
They were wizards.
We were in love and trouble.
We wanted salt peanuts,
pennies from heaven,
a love supreme,
a love supreme.

PRESSING FLATS

You wanna sleep on my chest?
You wanna listen to my heart beat
all through the night?
It's the only jazz station
with a twenty-four-hour signal,
if you wanna listen.

If you answer yes
I expect you to be able
to sleep in a pit of cobras.
You should be willing
to destroy your enemy
if it comes to that.
If you have a weapon,
if you know how to use your hands.

You should be able to distinguish
oppression from pleasure.
Some pleasure is oppression
but then, that isn't pleasure, is it?
Some drugs induce pleasure
but isn't that oppression?

If you're immobilized you're oppressed.
If you're killing yourself you're oppressed.
If you don't know who you are
you're pressed.

A prayer candle won't always solve the
        confusion,
the go-go won't always take the mind off things.
Our lives don't get better with coke,
they just—get away from us.

There doesn't have to be a bomb
if we make up our minds

we don't want to die that way.
We're told what's right from left.
We're told there is good and evil,
laws and punishment,
but no one speaks of the good in evil
or the evil in good.

You wanna sleep on my chest?
You wanna listen to my heart beat
all through the night?
It's the only jazz station
with a twenty-four-hour signal
if you wanna listen.
If you know what I mean.

IF HIS NAME WERE MANDINGO

He speaks good damn English to me.
I'm his brother, Carver.
He doesn't speak
that "dis" and "dat" bull
I've seen quoted.
Every word he speaks
rings clear in my head.
I don't suppose you ever
hear him clearly?
You're always busy,
seeking other things of him.
His name isn't important.
It would be coincidence
if he had a name,
a face, a mind.
If he's not hard-on
then he's hard up
and either way
you watch him.
You want crossover music.
You want his pleasure
without guilt or capture.
You don't notice
many things about him.
He doesn't always
wear a red ski cap,
eat fried chicken,
fuck like a jungle.
He doesn't always
live with his mother,
or off the street,
or off some bitch as you assume.
You give the appearance of concern.
You offer him twenty dollars
telling him it's cabfare
and discharge him from your home.

Your paths cross the next day.
You don't acknowledge him,
but he remembers,
his seed dilutes in your blood.
He doesn't dance well,
but you don't notice.
He's only visible
in the dark
to you.

BLACK BEANS

Times are lean,
Pretty Baby,
the beans are burnt
to the bottom
of the battered pot.
Let's make fierce love
on the overstuffed
hand-me-down sofa.
We can burn it up, too.
Our hungers
will evaporate like—money.
I smell your lust,
not the pot burnt black
with tonight's meager meal.
So we can't buy flowers for our table.
Our kisses are petals,
our tongues caress the bloom.
Who dares to tell us
we are poor and powerless?
We keep treasure
any king would count as dear.
Come on, Pretty Baby.
Our souls can't be crushed
like cats crossing streets too soon.
Let the beans burn all night long.
Our chipped water glasses are filled
with wine from our loving.
And the burnt black beans—
caviar.

HOMOCIDE

for Ronald Gibson

Grief is not apparel.
Not like a dress, a wig
or my sister's high-heeled shoes.
It is darker than the man I love
who in my fantasies comes for me
in a silver, six-cylinder chariot.
I walk the waterfront/curbsides
in my sister's high-heeled shoes.
Dreaming of him, his name
still unknown to my tongue.
While I wait for my prince to come
from every other man
I demand pay for my kisses.
I buy paint for my lips.
Stockings for my legs.
My own high-heeled slippers
and dresses that become me.
When he comes,
I know I must be beautiful.
I will know how to love his body.
Standing out here
on the waterfront/curbsides
I have learned to please
a man.
He will bring me flowers.
He will bring me silk
and jewels, I know.
While I wait,
I'm the only man who loves me.
They call me "Star"
because I listen
to their dreams and wishes.
But grief is darker.
It is a wig
that does not rest gently
on my head.

BETTER DAYS

In daytime hours
guided by instincts
that never sleep,
the faintest signals
come to me
over vast spaces
of etiquette
and restraint.
Sometimes I give in
to the pressing call of instinct,
knowing the code of my kind
better than I know
the National Anthem
or "The Lord's Prayer."
I am so driven by my senses
to abandon restraint,
to seek pure pleasure
through every pore.
I want to smell the air
around me thickly scented
with a playboy's freedom.
I want impractical relationships.
I want buddies and partners,
names I will forget by sunrise.
I don't want to commit my heart.
I only want to feel good.
I only want to freak sometimes.
There are no other considerations.
A false safety compels me
to think I will never need kindness,
so I don't recognize
that need in someone else.

But it concerns me,
going off to sleep
and waking

throbbing with wants,
that I am being
consumed by want.
And I wonder
where stamina comes from
to search all night
until my footsteps ring
awake the sparrows,
and I go home, ghost walking,
driven indoors to rest
my hunter's guise,
to love myself as fiercely
as I have in better days.

ALPHA WAVE DISRUPTIONS

Television is watching us.
Counting us like fingers.
While we sleep
our homelands disappear.
Urban pioneers plant
land mines beneath flower beds.
I bought a bomb downtown,
a kiss, some drugs,
all of this can kill.
The police stop me at a roadblock,
ask me: where I live?
I tell them anywhere I can—
off a bitch, on a bench, on a grate.
They want proof.
They arrest me for having none.
They suspect I'm a non-person.
I tell them I come from Earth.
They choke me at my collar
and tell me no such place exists.
They set bail for my life.
They assign my organs and brains
to the state.
They assign my flesh to a coat factory.
Satellites are listening to us.
We are never alone
but we are lonely and lonesome.
We are being watched by infrared eyes,
we are being listened to by sonar ears.
A microchip is more valuable than a heart.
And silicone doesn't bleed.

SURRENDER IS TREASON

I'm a desperate man.
I lock myself indoors at night.
I know the streets
will not be safe
if I walk.
I haven't killed anyone
or robbed anyone
or used any violence.
I am young enough
and black enough to be accused.
One lone soldier
guards my soul in the valley.
Satan watches that soldier.
Fear is the only grip
I have on sanity.
Fear of sirens
screaming to shatter
the night's delicate testicles.
Fear of bloody fangs.
Fear of smoking guns.
Fear of execution
by a state which pushes me
to the edge
like a crowd with pointed sticks
throwing rocks and bricks.
When I fall I will not die.
Only the promises I made as a citizen.

I am no longer a clear-thinking man.
My citizenship has always been questionable.
I hurt and ache and crave.
I can't cry.
I can't afford my addictions.
I make my weapons
out of what I find on the streets—
old umbrellas, loose tongues,

limbs of trees I sharpen into knives.
I'm a lean man, a man of color.
I waste the meaning of foolishness like seed.
My youth is against me and for me.
It can make me a profit or a criminal.
I could sell myself to you but
I don't want to compromise anymore.
I don't want to sleep anymore.
I don't want to beg, but I have begged.
I don't want sympathy—
there is no ego left to appreciate it.

I don't want to rape.
I don't want to kill.
I don't want to lie.
I don't want to cheat and steal.
I don't want to spill blood, but I must ...
I don't want to run, but if I must ...
Satan watches me like a vulture.
I'm fucking the Angel of Death.
I don't dream because dreams make me hungry.
I'm young enough, black enough
to be shot on sight, questioned later.
I am a son. My life is a hunter's season.
Dark men, men of color
must always be alert.
Surprise is life costing.
Surrender is treason.

FOREVER

Even hope is a device.

         I will never come back.
I'm sent below Earth
to violate its intestines.
The bosses teach me to steal
but kill me when I do so for myself.
I'm given a torch. A lantern.
The rock I chip is as hard as my heart.
My pick is loneliness, chipping, chipping.

         I will never come back to daylight.
The lanterns make me loneliest of all.
I want from my brother what I need from a
       woman.
I will die, my lungs congested
with filaments of power that don't serve me.

If I had a brick
and fast legs.
If I had a gun.
If I were an army.

STATE OF THE ART

I have only been here a week.
I almost don't belong.
I slipped through.
I came during the night.
I have a room in the center of town.

Whatever dreams I had coming here
seem suddenly dangerous under foot.
        Do I start again
to blow glass into another replica of worship?
If so, then I ask as a young man who is skeptical:
how do you blow life into glass? And when you
            do,
should you stand like the Piper of Hamelin,
or like Patton in the drilling yard at dawn,
or like Dizzy, under a waterfall of perspiration,
his cheeks puffed, black, sails.

DRINKIN

Seven flat rum & cokes
egyptian wine
ju ju juice
terror water
in twelve-ounce cans.
It makes you feel more of a man.
It gives you kinship
with losers and escapists.
So blind you can't recall
ancient evenings, rose petals
or where you put the keys
to your pyramid.
In the parks, where there should be
statues standing in your honor,
instead your bodies are strewn about
in disruption,
connected to nothing in this world,
a park littered with innocent men.

So while Cook was over at Loop Loop
drinkin snake-head juice with Ro Ro,
Roxanne left a long letter
telling Cook she wouldn't return
to pick up after him again
like a brokenhearted barmaid.

We drinkin y'all.
Seven flat rum & cokes
egyptian wine
ju ju juice
terror water.

Temptations play on the juke box.
I want to hold a woman.
I want to hold a man.
This old heart of mine shouldn't be so kind.

I should put you out of your misery,
interfere with God's work.

And the letter went on and on
like a blues song,
a passing midnight train.

Cook was over at Loop Loop
drinkin jungle juice with Ro Ro.
You could call them brothers
in an extended misery.
Hit a B-flat and think of them.
But all I want
is a statue in the park.
Something honorable and dignified for them.
But inscribe it with excerpts
from Roxanne's letter.
A memorial
for the carnage
of domestic war.

LE SALON

Lowering my pants
before another mouth;
the cheap movie reel
rattles in its compartment
while the silent color movie
for a quarter
grinds around and around.
We pant in a dark booth.
The musk of hair
burns our nostrils.
I moan as his mouth
swallows me.
This is the first sound
in this silent movie.
Then he moans
giving the movie
its dialogue.

UNDER CERTAIN CIRCUMSTANCES

I am lonely for past kisses,
for wild lips certain streets
breed for pleasure.
Romance is a foxhole.
This kind of war frightens me.
I don't want to die
sleeping with soldiers
I don't love.

I want to court outside the race,
outside the class, outside the attitudes—
but love is a dangerous word
in this small town.
Those who seek it are sometimes found
facedown floating on their beds.
Those who find it protect it
or destroy it from within.

But the disillusioned—
those who've lost the stardust,
the moondance, the waterfront;
like them, I long for my past.
When I was ten, thirteen, twenty—
I wanted candy, five dollars, a ride.

WHERE SEED FALLS

Stalking.
The neighborhood is dangerous
but we go there.
We walk the long way.
Our jangling keys
mute the sound of our stalking.
To be under the sky, above
or below a man.
This is our heat.
Radiant in the night.
Our hands blister with semen.
A field of flowers blossoms
where we gather
in empty warehouses.
Our seed falls
without the sound or
grace of stars.
We lurk in shadows.
We are the hunger of shadows.
In the dark
we don't have to say
I love you.
The dark swallows it
And sighs like we sigh,
when we rise
from our knees.

O TELL ME, BRUTUS

O tell me, Brutus,
with corpses decomposing
in the river,
loved ones keeping fevers
quiet in city hospitals,
the backrooms, locked and chained,
the police with new power to seize
and search our hearts, our kisses,
our mutual consents around midnight.

O tell me, Brutus,
what are we to do
with all this leather,
all these whips and chains?

NOW WE THINK

Now we think
as we fuck
this nut
might kill us.
There might be
a pin-sized hole
in the condom.
A lethal leak.

We stop kissing
tall dark strangers,
sucking mustaches,
putting lips
tongues
everywhere.
We return to pictures.
Telephones.
Toys.
Recent lovers.
Private lives.

Now we think
as we fuck
this nut might kill.
This kiss could turn
to stone.

BALLOONS

In black plastic bags
tied at the top
they were buried.
Their faces
swollen with death
rise in my dreams.
I was seventeen
when I read of them:
young boys, young men
lured to a house in Texas.
Their penises were filled
with excited blood:
first hard then soft they became
as Death with its blistered lips
kissed them one by one.
They were grapes
on Death's parched tongue.
In plastic bags
tied at the top
they were buried.
Twenty-five of them
and more unclaimed
young boys, young men.
For a long time
I retreated to women.
But it was like dancing
following a pattern of steps
painted on the floor.
Now, the awkward dancing is over.

For three days
I have walked
by a dark gray house
at the end of my street
where lives a man
out of whose home I have seen

young boys, young men
coming and going
coming and going.

And for three days,
from the second-floor windows,
music from dusk to dusk
has fallen like petals
of black roses
softly to the ground.

But tonight,
evening of the third day,
I call the police
and tell them
not about faces
rising like balloons.
I will tell them instead
about music,
about petals from black roses
falling softly to the ground.
Perhaps they will understand.
Maybe they will
come to my street
and knock at the door
of the gray house,
where lives this man
I have not seen
for three days,
whose face is beginning to rise
in my dreams
like balloons.

ISN'T IT FUNNY

I don't want to hear you beg.
I'm sick of beggars.
If you a man
take what you want from me
or what you can.
Even if you have me
like some woman across town
you think you love.

Look at me
standing here with my dick
as straight as yours.
What do you think this is?
The weather cock on a rooftop?

We sneak all over town
like two damn thieves
whiskey on our breath,
no streetlights on the back roads,
just the stars above us
as ordinary as they should be.

We always have to work it out,
walk it through, talk it over,
drink and smoke our way into sodomy.
I could take you in my room
but you're afraid the landlady
will recognize you.
I feel thankful I don't love you.
I won't have to suffer you later on.

But for now I say, Johnnie Walker,
have you had enough, Johnnie Walker?
Do-I-look-like-a-woman-now?
Against the fogged car glass
do I look like your crosstown lover?

Do I look like Shirley?

When you reach to kiss her lips
they're thick like mine.
Her hair is cut close, too,
like mine—
isn't it?

THE EDGE

I

I should have loved him forever
or put a bullet in his muthafuckin' head.

II

The past has made me
a good lover and a whore,
placed me closer to my fantasies
of being a beautiful Japanese boy.
My worldly charms exclusively sought
by the connoisseurs of freak,
who worldwide know
I keep a small apartment
in a reputable neighborhood.
I am quietly kept
in a style
befitting a child of wealth.
If youth were longer
I could enter my manhood
a gentleman of nobility.
But instead I fight
with others like myself
for attention
I once squandered,
because I could not count
the minutes my youth
would sacrifice on vanity.
I exalted myself in a mirror.
Narcissus would have wanted
to see me reflected.
So now, in a high-rise sympathy
I give myself
in foolishly thought
charity to men,

who are but mere reflections
of the die-hard dreams
I pass on to begging boys
whose names I forget
for the convenience
forgetting gives me.

Behind a wall of mirrors
I tell my skeleton of youth
I am beautiful.
I will endure.

III

You left me begging for things
some men thought they had
below their belts.
I was reaching higher.
I could throw my legs up
like satellites, but I knew
I was fucking fallen angels.
I made them feel like demigods.
I believed my mission
to be a war zone duty:
don't create casualties,
heal them.
But I was the wounded,
the almost dead,
helping the uninjured.
Men whose lusty hearts weakened
in the middle of the night,
and brought them to tears,
to their knees
for their former lovers.
They could look at me and tell
they did not want to endure

what beauty love scars give me.
So touch me now—
Hannibal, Toussaint.
I am a revolution without bloodshed.
I change the order of things
to suit my desperations.
You can raise your legs,
almost touch heaven.
I can be an angel
falling.

BETWEEN PATHOS AND SEDUCTION

for Larry

Love potions
solve no mysteries,
provide no comment
on the unspoken.
Our lives tremble
between pathos and seduction.
Our inhibitions
force us to be equal.
We swallow hard
black love potions
from a golden glass.
New language beckons us.
Its dialect present.
Intimate.
Through my eyes
focused as pure, naked light,
fixed on you like magic,
clarity. I see risks.
Regrets? There will be none.
Let some wonder,
some worry some accuse.
Let you and I know
the tenderness
only we can bear.

HEAVY CORNERS

for Joe

Don't let it be loneliness
that kills us.
If we must die
on the front line
let us die men
loved by both sexes.

Don't let it be envy
that drives us
to suck our thumbs
or shoot each other dead
over snake eyes.

Let us not be dancing
with the wind
on heavy corners
tattered by doom.

Let us not accept
partial justice.
If we believe our lives
are priceless
we can't be conquered.

If we must die
on the front line
don't let loneliness
kill us.

EQUUS

The suspect
is in his early twenties.
a marine.
perversely sensitive g.i. joe doll
factory boxed.   battery operated.
remote controlled.
     given guns
bombs   tear gas.
an indiscreet license to kill anything
which threatens the state.
trained to live for this country,
these soldiers who stiffen
at the sound of a man's command.
these macho boys
clean-cut   disciplined machines
hurl bricks and tear gas
into public gatherings of civilian men.
what do they fear?
if the men hold hands and dance
the world will not end.
if they love and part with the seasons
are they communists?
anarchists perhaps?
leftist urban guerrillas?
sexual terrorists?
do you fear their lovers
will snap their minds
and they'll go off killing
little boys in revenge?
just what is it g.i. joe?
is this the retaliation
of scorned love?

ROMANCE IS INTRIGUE
for Alexis

Amid conflicting reports
the truth emerges.
Coarse edged.
An ungentle blade.
For peeling back
the night's skin.
In no way an easy task.
It requires great strength
in the hands. A strength
not as obvious as muscles.
So I watch you.
Through the eyes
of people I love.
The good and the bad
they tell me, I hear.
I believe what I feel
moves unsaid in the air
between us.
This is not like trains
or lunch or gossip.
A brownstone gapped-tooth
griot girl like you
should understand.
This is not via satellite.
My arms are still attached
but empty.
You do not lay slain
in a lover's ambush.
Amid conflicting reports.
Satellite blackouts.
It is true.
Some of the people we love
are terrorists.

AMERICAN WEDDING

In america,
I place my ring
on your cock
where it belongs.
No horsemen
bearing terror,
no soldiers of doom
will swoop in
and sweep us apart.
They're too busy
looting the land
to watch us.
They don't know
we need each other
critically.
They expect us to call in sick,
watch television all night,
die by our own hands.
They don't know
we are becoming powerful.
Every time we kiss
we confirm the new world coming.

What the rose whispers
before blooming
I vow to you.
I give you my heart,
a safe house.
I give you promises other than
milk, honey, liberty.
I assume you will always
be a free man with a dream.
In america,
place your ring
on my cock

where it belongs.
Long may we live
to free this dream.

IN THE LIFE

Mother, do you know
I roam alone at night?
I wear colognes,
tight pants, and
chains of gold,
as I search
for men willing
to come back
to candlelight.

I'm not scared of these men
though some are killers
of sons like me. I learned
there is no tender mercy
for men of color,
for sons who love men
like me.

Do not feel shame for how I live.
I chose this tribe
of warriors and outlaws.
Do not feel you failed
some test of motherhood.
My life has borne fruit
no woman could have given me
anyway.

If one of these thick-lipped,
wet, black nights
while I'm out walking,
I find freedom in this village.
If I can take it with my tribe
I'll bring you here.
And you will never notice
the absence of rice
and bridesmaids.

THREAD

Trying not to think of you
yet your face colors
every contour
of my mind.
And every way I turn
inside of a minute
I collide
with your laughter.
I am wind,
and you
are chimes.

[EX-BOXER. RETIRED FROM THE RING.]

Ex-boxer. Retired from the ring.
Heart complications. Head injuries.
It cost to be a champion.

A sleek scar slashed above your eye.
Left side. From a jab
full of thirty-two stitches.
Concussion.

You worked for the church
while I knew you.
There you taught me
romance and seduction.
It was our first meeting.
I had phoned the church
to speak to the Reverend.
You answered.
He wasn't in ...

For two years
I was hot and nervous
about sodomizing an angel
in the church.
You locked us in a room
I never wanted to leave.

I didn't worry about my conduct,
minister's son that I am.
It was impossible to be sacrilegious.
I felt beautiful for the first time.
I slept upon your back
spent, peaceful;
a canopy of spring above
an autumn of discontent.

What the seasons leave me now
I understand because I choose
to remember the splendid lights
of secrecy and magic.
You took fear from me.
My innocence. My bittersweet.

What the seasons leave—
seed, buds, blossoms, stalks.
The seeds are impotent.
The buds are crisp.
The blossoms brown delicate whispers.
The stalks once green and sweet
could poison.

With what the seasons leave
I assemble memory.
I recall you were a champion.
Invisible scars disfigured you.
You revealed them.
I didn't know then
what I was seeing
until now —
in the late inclement spring
as my discontent
flourishes.

32 bearded.
37, f/a, gk/passive, 165 lbs.
49 a muscular bottom.
25 uninhibited.
52 prefers french tongues, whippings, hand
        beatings.
35 has toys for boys.
22 is uncut and new to the scene.
29 needs a little bowl to put some sugar in.
prefer black bottoms, big balls, buns well done.
no s&m, fats, fems, no fist-fucking.
tired of baths bars bushes bookstores beating off.
must be very horny, very hung, very young.
wish to quietly court, date adonis, lick leather.
Dial 338 late at night you can call I'm a number.

WHAT TWENTY CENTS WILL GET YOU

You have his heart to eat.
Shards of glass you swallow
but your sleep is still disturbed.

You dream of radiant flowers
with glistening teeth that bloom
only at night. I have his flesh
from time to time.
I'm a man eater.
That used to be taboo.

I don't hold an uzi to his head
threatening to kill him.
His clothes peel off without my help—
they just slip away.

He's not the man I want
to spend my life with.
I only want to suck his cock,
give him what he's not getting
at home.
I don't want to eat his heart,
you can choke on it alone.

He carried himself
like an available man,
a man for a minute or two.

He called you a woman
he doesn't love,
a woman he'll never marry.
But now that we've met,
your baritone voice
and bearded face reveal
no womanly charm.

You threaten my life —
hinting at disaster.
If you want to be a hero
if you want to risk dying
do so with significance.
You so bad
you so bad
you so bad
go kill Botha.

Otherwise your man
isn't worth dying for.
I haven't had him
all over town,
but others have.
Others will.

[AND WHEN I GET HOT FOR YOU]

And when I get hot for you
I close my eyes,
pretend I'm a virgin.
I replace what I didn't know then
with cruelties I know now.
I ride you all around the world.
I use my tongue like a weapon.
I want you to surrender.
Please, baby.
The floor is outerspace.
We fall there
clinging to each other.
On another planet,
looking up at us,
we're a double rainbow
in the sky.
We're the sunset
of another ordinary day.

[LOVE POTIONS]

Love potions
solve no mysteries,
provide no comment on the unspoken.
Our lives tremble
between pathos and seduction.
Our inhibitions force us to be equal.
We swallow hard
black love potions
from a golden glass.
New language beckons us.
Its dialect present.
Intimate.
Through my eyes
focused as pure, naked light,
fixed on you like magic,
clarity.
I see risks.
Regrets?
There will be none.
Let some wonder, some worry, some accuse.
Let you and I know the tenderness
only we can bear.

[WHAT WILL BE BOMBED TODAY?]

What will be bombed today?
American Cafe at noon?
A playground of nappy head?
Do you dread
your house will cinder
and firemen will stand around
watching the block
burn to the ground
like a Salem witch,
a nigga in a tree?
Do you see?
Do you dread?
Do the papers panic you?
Do you sleep with a gun
beneath your pillow?
What will be bombed today?
Rosslyn Tunnel?
The A uptown?
Another funeral in Soweto?
An abortion clinic?

AMERICAN FAMILY, 1984

If there were seven blind men
one of them unable to hear
would be father.
He would be the one
promising to deliver
what never arrives.
He is the bridge
which on one side
I stand feeling doomed
to never forgive him
for the violence in our past,
while on the other side
he vigorously waves to me
to cross over,
but he doesn't know
the bridge has fallen through.

If there were seven blind men
the deaf one would be father.
The mute, his son.

VOWS

for Mel

Moon of the ragged sunbirds,
of the fermenting grapes,
of the dark wood I have polished
and polished all afternoon.
To make wine of these things,
to make lace of stones,
to give you all rain becomes
after it falls throughout summer,
knowing these to be small, trifle gifts.
Bunches of flowers, stalks of corn,
even trees and delicate roses redder than my
          blood,
redder than two bloods running together,
redder than the lips of a woman of tragedy.

I bring you the moon of the ragged sunbirds,
the jewel crusted with my sorrows,
the hands of a gray morning to soften the jewel,
and toll the bells, and toll the bells.

"U.S. PLANNING TO WAGE WAR IN SPACE"
—*The Washington Post* 1/10/77

We have yet
to correctly name
all the wreckage.

Some still wait in line
for their elbows,
for their fingers
that once wore wedding rings,
for the speech to sprout
in their throats again
like buds on a barren bush.

We have yet to bear sons
in the gaps
and in the silences of misplaced fathers.

There is loose talk
of arming the contellations
with machine guns,
of digging trenches
in clusters of stars.

The plans call
for camouflaging the planets.
Even the docile moon
must make a decision
to move right
or left.

CHANCES ARE FEW

I eat no meat.
I have no wishbones.
I am too urban
To know of rootworking.
There are no witch doctors
living in my neighborhood.
I look up at the stars at night
and think they are too small
to bear the weight of what I wish for.
I know no woman named Zora
whom I can take my palms to.
And this morning,
I washed your comb.
I have none of your hair
to save in a small box.

AFTER SCHOOL

I am trying to spell the boy's name
with his spelling blocks.
I am trying to write my own
in my infant hand.
I am trying to cradle this baby.
When I hold the boy
I raise the weight of a sledgehammer
over our heads.
One month old and he dares
to break my back.

Your skirts were easier to lift
rustling like feathers of swans.

This is your father's marriage.
The shabby grace your mother displays
for the public eye.
A name for this boy.
The absence of love
as startling as his cry for your breasts.

I lie beside you at night
wishing death to come.

I can't sleep.
I can't lift the boy into my arms.
We will escape.
By my hand I can make us fugitives.
I watch you fall onto the kitchen floor.
I hear your skirts falling like evening on the sky.
I go over to the boy's crib. As I aim at his head,
as it shatters, I see your father's and mother's
        faces.
They can't arrest us again for our passion,
for the innocence of our mouths
following our fingertips.

And the boy, into him
all my dreams slipped like the canes of old men.
He is the evidence I destroy.
That my thighs ever throbbed for you,
that your hard, pointed nipples stabbed my
       tongue,
that our deaths were prior to the gunshot
       wounds,
by the repeated blows of a sledgehammer.

OBSERVATION IN A WAR ZONE

Nightly, in glinting handcuffs
or under bloody sheets,
a parade of Black men
marches across my TV screen.
On every channel
the news is dominated
by Black men
or descriptions of them,
wanted for murder,
robbery, rape,
or suspicion.
Young, bloodthirsty
drug turks
feed the news pictures
of daily death and warfare.
Destruction assumes
Negroid features,
as does genocide,
sorrow, and fear.

CONFESSIONS OF A MASK

I was one of the children.
I was up and coming and legendary.
I worked for a place of honor within my tribe,
a trophy I could take home to mother.
I was not ashamed of what I was,
the subtle mutations identity underwent;
subtle to me simply because I didn't want to see
flaws and imperfections in what was inevitably
man-made—a ceremonial mask for my naked
      heart,
a tattered, floral, springtime dress for my soul.

I have been a pussy and a dick, a cunt, a cock.
I have bent gender to the will of my needs
and they were not always selfish needs,
there were always others to consider,
their satisfaction, their pleasure,
the quality of their desire.

Restrictions were there, limits plain enough
to see, there was always death nearby—
it became the constant in our lives
while we were still young and virile.
Death as crime, death as entertainment, death
from neglect, denial, disillusionment, disease.
I let myself go rather cheaply,
too afraid to articulate the loneliness
that killed a few of my brothers
as they slept dreaming of all kinds of freedom.
I lived for more than the next dick.

Now that I no longer confuse sex with love,
it is easier to sleep alone
and live my days
accountable for my decisions.

Now that I see the difference
between pleasure and commitment,
moving through what could be
my middle years or my final years—
I don't know, I try not to think
about which it will be.

But when they ask, later on,
tell them I was a hot fuck,
a freaky fuck, a delightful fuck.
Tell them I kept myself
ready for anything ...

IF WE CAN'T BE INSTRUCTED BY GRIEF

—for Washington, D.C.

Living on the rough edges of a diamond,
filaments of refracted light cut.
Seeking peace that eludes capture.
Paying daily for the search.
Alleviate this tax burden upon spirit—
all winter we've been smelling blood,
tracking murder. The foul breath
of death is everywhere.

Welcome to Washington, D.C.
home of rock stars,
go-go bands, stick-up boys,
and Bonnie and Clyde couples
cruising in paid-for-with-cash BMWs.
Living like death has no impact
on their conscience.
How will we share the future
if we cannot be instructed by grief?

Living like this costs
a little bit of something:
A pint of blood.
A bit of evaporated trust.
Three kilos of corruption.

A spoon of spite,
a spate of sex crimes,
a box of dead infant flakes.
Mix in a large bowl
and serve at parties,
on lunch hours,
on street corners,
in school yards;
listen for the bullets
to start popping.

Welcome to Washington, D.C.,
Rock Capital of the World.
See the corpses and carnage?
Don't flinch. Don't scream.
Someone will know you're a tourist.

I live in a town
where it's easier to get crack
than it is to get food,
easier to get a grave
than it is to get shelter,
a town, where
the infant mortality rates
read like the statistics
for an underdeveloped country.

I'm concerned. I'm scared. I vote.
I pray. The police say
my fear is "drug-related."
They wear yellow rubber gloves
because it's contagious.
They cordon off Black neighborhoods
to keep it from spreading.

Open-air drug markets
outnumber the combined total
of area supermarkets
by three to one.
But we District residents
have yet to blame
the complicity of our silence
and the needs of our addictions
for the blood flowing in the streets.

Welcome to Washington, D.C.,
an international Murder Capital

perched beside the Potomac
and Anacostia rivers.
A funk song once proclaimed D.C.
"Chocolate City"
because of its large Black population,
but lately, residents are heard saying
D.C. is "Dodge City" or "The Wild Wild West"
which frightens them more than corruption.

DEADLY WEAPONS

In my loneliest gestures
learning to live
with less is less.
I never wanted
to be your son.
You never made the choice
to be my father.
What we have learned
from no textbook—
how to live
without one another,
how to evade
the stainless truth,
how to store our waste
in tombs beneath the heart,
knowing at any moment
it could leak out.
Do we expect to survive?
What are we prepared for?
Trenched off,
communications down,
angry in alien tongues.
We use extreme weapons
to ward off one another.
Some nights
our opposing reports
are heard as we dream.
Silence is
our deadliest weapon.
We both use it.
Precisely.
Often.

MEDITATIONS IN A WAR ZONE

What we are attempting is dangerous:
Building a bridge.
Forging a bond.
Helping one another.
Let no one sway us otherwise.
We must keep on loving each other
through the killings.

It is not a singing circle of protest,
nor an embrace of mourning
or celebration I speak of.
We are not simply summoning
ancestral powers,
nor casting spells
to cure our troubles.
This is not a circle jerk
of gorgeous, frightened men.
We do not come together
to entertain you—
we've done enough of that,
and still, we're disrespected,
our brilliance all but denied
and sabotaged.

This is not a circle
formed for reflection:
Mirror mirror on the wall
How long does it take
To grow blonde, Nordic and tall?
That is not my question
not at all,
not at all.

Someone, gently, rock a Black man.
Comfort him. Someone please
please be brave enough

to hold him back from extinction.
Hold his hands
against self-destruction.
Tell him he is beautiful.
Tell him you love him.

What if all Black men
across varied differences
agreed to pray in unison
for the American Bald Eagles
to drop dead,
so we can claim priority
as an "Endangered Species."
And if the bald eagles
did drop dead,
think of what we might
pray for next,
what
kind of meditation
on history
it would be,
what angels would descend
in haste to do
our specific bidding;
think of what we might pray for
in unison, Black men,
and never stop.

We must keep on loving each other
through the killings,
the secret meetings,
the skin-bleaching commercials,
the charts and graphs
we cannot see.
The National Rifle Association
lobbies for our deaths.

Remember this, when they contribute
to the campaigns of our elected officials.
Remember this, when public hospitals
cannot care for the wounded and critical,
and they shut their doors
and lock them
in the middle of a war zone
we once called home.

SULTAN

He penetrated every chamber,
storing himself inside me,
in every cell and follicle,
in every pimple and artery,
he established residence
to be recalled in my dreams
or summoned by my hand.

THE PERFECT MOMENT
for Robert Mapplethorpe

Aesthetics can justify desire,
but desire in turn
can provoke punishment.
Under public scrutiny
the eyes of one man
are focused on another.
Is it desire, equality,
disgust, or hatred?
Is the quality of loneliness
present or overlooked?
Is it diminished
by the breaking of taboos?
Is the passion mutual
or is one wary of
the other?
Does fear haunt the edges
of the photographs?
Does it blaze inside the cornea
or lurk like men in shadows
posed for the perfect moment
to snap or strike or sigh?

BLUE RINSE

I wanted some hair like Ethel's
so I went running downtown
on that raggedy-assed A2
one Saturday morning.
I couldn't get none
of my Southeast girlfriends
to drive me downtown,
they were too busy
laying up or lying low.

So the bus got me downtown
it seemed like a damn day later.
I marched into Woolworth's
and strolled on up to the wig counter.
This thin, nervous little clerk
slouched on over and asked me:
"Well what can I do for you in here today?"
I ignored her tone and said:
I need some of Ethel's hair.
I need waves of it falling
all around my face,
I want to pile it high on my head.

The clerk bent down behind the counter
to get me this
dusty pink and black hatbox.
When I opened it,
there was a long
braided blonde wig inside.
I said look here, Sweetie,
you might need this kind of help
and some more,
but I don't
need no blonde wig.
Now I don't know
what you're trying to signify,

but I said Ethel's hair
will do just fine.

Then I pointed to a wig stand
holding a shoulder length
wool-curled mane of black hair.
I want to frame my face
in hair like that,
hair someone might feel
like writing a song for,
hair someone might want
to shake awake and play with
instead of rushing off
in the dawn like a thief.
I want hair from here to there,
and I pointed from the wig counter
to the door.
I said if Ethel can have hair
on her head
from her eyebrows
to the floor
and she's bald as a chicken, too,
then I know I can have me some hair
from over yonder
to over there.

Now I swear, girl,
you must be a little deaf and dumb
if you don't know what I mean.
I don't want no red hair,
no bush hair, no blue hair—
that black will do just fine.
I want that hair
to be mine right now.
I want a crown of glory
every eye will envy.

Don't trouble yourself
putting it in no box,
I'll wear it out—yes indeed, Lord.
This hair like Ethel's hair
is gonna blow in the breeze,
tease and please,
it's gonna come alive on my head.
It's gonna cover those rocks
crowding me out of my bed
because my crying
hasn't softened them
at all.

THE EMPEROR'S CLOTHES

So let us sleep.
Let me cover you in my sheets.
Pretend they are the finely woven silks of a king.
I have a kingdom if I have you. It is not
palm wine telling me to say this. They call you
my boy in the village. They speak of my many
sleeveless robes. They call me cutsleeves.
So many mornings I have left you sleeping
to attend to court and duties
with one sleeve on my robe
the other under your head.
But no matter the busy tongues nor duty
our peace is not disturbed.
Let them say what they will.
I have many tailors
to mend what none can wear.

THE BRASS RAIL

CALL	I saw you last night
RESPONSE	Many occupants are never found.
CALL	in the basement
RESPONSE	Many canoes overturn.
CALL	of the Brass Rail.
RESPONSE	Your dark diva's face, a lake
CALL	Lushing and laughing.
RESPONSE	I hear the sea
CALL	Your voice falling from the air.
RESPONSE	screaming behind your eyes.
CALL	Dancing with the boys on the edge of funk.
RESPONSE	Twilight.
CALL	The boys danced, darling,
RESPONSE	My tongue
CALL	touching you indiscreetly.
RESPONSE	walks along your thighs like a hermit.
CALL	Your body a green light
RESPONSE	I have been naked with you.
CALL	urging them to be familiar.
RESPONSE	Dear Diva, Darling:
CALL	You were in the mirrors, the light. Their arms.
RESPONSE	The boys whispered about you
CALL	and singapore slings toasted you.
RESPONSE	under the music pumping from the jukebox.
CALL	They were promises chilled by ice cubes
RESPONSE	They were promises chilled by ice cubes.
CALL	The boys whispered about you
RESPONSE	The sloe gin fizzes
CALL	under the music pumping from the jukebox.

RESPONSE	and singapore slings toasted you.
CALL	You were in the mirrors/the light. Their arms.
RESPONSE	Your body a green light urging them to be familiar.
CALL	Dear Diva, Darling:
RESPONSE	The boys danced, darling,
CALL	I have been naked with you.
RESPONSE	touching you indiscreetly.
CALL	My tongue has walked along your thighs like a hermit.
RESPONSE	Dancing on the edge of funk.
CALL	I have found the scent. Twilight.
RESPONSE	Your voice falling from the air.
CALL	I hear the sea screaming behind your eyes.
RESPONSE	Lushing and laughing.
CALL	Your dark diva's face,
RESPONSE	I saw you last night
CALL	a lake.
RESPONSE	in the basement
CALL	Many canoes overturn.
RESPONSE	of the Brass Rail
CALL	Many occupants are never found.

MEDITATIONS

P.S. P.S. P.S.
DEAR MUTHAFUCKIN DREAMS.
WHAT'S THE MATTER
WITH THESE GODDAMN MIRACLES TODAY?
THEY DON'T APPEAR FRESH.
THEY LOOK THAWED OUT,
GLASSY-EYED, MARKED DOWN.
WHO WANTS THESE
SHABBY-ASSED MIRACLES?
WHO CAN BE SAVED
BY THESE SHADOWS OF OFFERING?
WHO CAN LAST A DAY
ON THIS?

SUGA', SUGA'

A few nights ago
I was deep sucking your dick
sucking your dick deep
like a thirsty person
devouring nectar in a desert,
an animal devouring blood.
Sucking.   Sucking.
I believed it all a mirage
that had conspiratorially engaged
my body and its senses.
I am numb with slaughter.
I can't bear another death
on my block, in my building,
around the corner.
What I want has to be
hotter than a blood fight,
crueler than a cutting duel.

A few nights ago I was
gnashing around on my bed
like an animal that needed
to be tranquilized
or shot in the head.
I was terrorizing
too many suburban living
rooms and crowded city flats.
Everything has a time line
to decipher.   I have a mission.
I have already lived beyond torture,
enduring the sadism of my masters
and the jealousy of the other slaves.
I let the timeline
remain undecipherable
and claim beyond prophecies
my destiny from the
fierce gale winds

disclaiming the ghetto streets.
I whistle of gunfire
and sirens.   I whistle
the troubles
of my brother and me.

A few nights ago
I wanted someone like you—

a wild lover,
big hands, huge feet,
a vital heart the cynicisms
of a common loneliness
cannot purge.
I wanted to be a flame,
sought after, believed.
I wanted to be more than a man
in drag as a ghetto girl.
I wanted simpler pleasures
that couldn't be written out
like a list of things.
I wanted the essence of abomination
and the boiling acidic spit
on the floor of your mouth
to dissolve my soul like suga'.
Suga'.

BLACK QUEEN

I'm an oversexed
well-hung
Black Queen
influenced
by phrases like
"the repetition
of beauty."

And you want me to sing
"We Shall Overcome?"
Do you daddy daddy
do you want me to coo
for your approval?
Do you want me
to squeeze my lips together
and suck you in?
Will I be a "brother" then?

I'm an oversexed
well-hung
Black Queen
influenced
by phrases like
"The love that dares
to speak its name."

And you want me to sing
"We Shall Overcome?"
Do you daddy daddy
do you want me to coo
for your approval?

Do you want me
to squeeze my lips together
and suck you in?
Will I be "visible" then?

I'm an oversexed
well-hung
Black Queen
influenced
by phrases like
"Silence equals death."

VITAL SIGNS

1
Erection my downfall,
as opposed to my rise.

2
You are so young
in my hands,
the gossip
of my neighbors
so true.

3
The police found him
with his dick
wickedly hacked off
and stuffed into his mouth.

Impossible for him
to answer their questions.
Impossible to tell them
who did it.

4
The shiny knife
clatters
to the floor
as you undress,
cutting the air
as it falls.
The blade: longer
than any dick
I've ever wanted.
I quickly
put my clothes
back on
and leave

the two of you
alone.

5

Beside the Schuylkill River,
near the Philadelphia Art Museum,
a calla lily is in bloom
                in a thicket
draped in gloom.
Its long pistil dangles down
swollen full of nectar.
A swarm of black bees
buzzes in the moonlight.

6

A flock of queens
gather on the corner.
A line of cars
snake around the block.

7

These bejeweled
exotic birds
preening
                and trilling
on the corner
are in danger,
even those
with talons.

8

This is the edge
society leaves them
to live on:
a lacerated,
lawless curbside

to click down
after midnight.
A cluster
       of shadows
lined with
car seats,
alleys,
bushes,
secretive
doorways
indistinguishable
from clusters
of ink blots.

9

At the bathhouse,
the thin white towel
loosely tied around
his dark waist
barely conceals
the excitement
I anticipate.

10

He stands before me,
lean, unshielded warrior.
I drop my thin white towel
to the floor, so he can see
I am also not afraid.

11

The two Black beauties
sculpted the length
of my white-sheeted bed,
are so still

in the moonlight
spilling through
tall windows,
lingering over them,
curious about their peace.

12
Hard to imagine them
anywhere else
for anyone's eyes
other than my own.
Hard to imagine
any other blessing
I care about more
at this moment.

13
Thankful for my eyes
I can see
their awesome beauty,
I can see them
in my rooms this way.
Thankful for my rooms—
they are safe.
Thankful for my bed—
wide enough for three.

14
The kiss I give his mouth
is passed on to his mouth
and his mouth then
returns it
to mine
to bloom.

15

I tell myself
I can't sit here
too long,
but I remain
in his lap
all night.

16

I offer you
the only leverage
I possess:
a strong
stern tool.

Take it!

Use it
for anything
but raping,
anything
but killing.

17

I am sure,
as I lower your legs
from my shoulders,
we will do this again
in the near future.

18

All afternoon
I am your lover.
You can keep me
until we expire
of old age,

ambush,
or disease.

19

At the threshold
of synthesis
I feel brave enough
   to surrender
not in a game
   of conquest,
but one of truth
and consequences.

20

I risk
hidden masks,
silent fears,
secret passageways.
Distance
suspended between us
like particles of air
and pollen.

21

This cloak we share.
The bed for our embracing.
The glass of wine
to sweeten our mouths
before we kiss.
I would tell no court
I am not familiar
with these things.
But if you ask me
not to
I will not say
you know them
as well as I.

CONSIDERATIONS

1

Be careful with your life
even when risk seems minimal.
Be careful with your trust
even when love is being claimed.
Be careful to speak exactly what you mean,
lucidness is the first step in becoming.
Honor your every loyalty,
the first being to yourself.

2

The important victory
of the day begins
at your bedside,
the moment you
regain consciousness,
the moment you
touch the floor,
breathe the air
of this reality,
against all sorts of odds
you rise. You win.
What victory
will you claim next?

3

Remember to always
give thanks
to your Creator.
To say thanks
is as divine
as forgiving.

4

Consider hatred
to be this:
the absence of everything.

5

If you are seeking discord
as a life path
my prayers for peace
go with you,
hunting dogs
snarling at your trail.

6

If you are jealous
of your friends
and neighbors
your garden
must be rotting
from lack of attention.

7

If you are envious
of others
it would seem
you possess
very little love
for yourself.

8

Faith kept
is a mighty power.
Cultivate power.
Cultivate faith.

9

If you are not
taking care
of your blessings
it will be obvious.

10

I should have looked at my horoscope
as closely as I read stock quotes
                this morning.
I should have followed my instincts,
the itch in my hand, the chill in my bones.
I should have gulped holy water for breakfast
instead of frozen, concentrated orange juice.
How can I possibly divine my purpose
if you continue to elude me.
Whether or not you realize it yet,
I am the prince who has come
to ride off with you
into the bullet-riddled sunset.
Down these ghetto streets we'll go
with destiny and undertow.

11

We started out as fuck buddies.
Now, occasionally, we make love.

AFTERWORD by John Keene

In preparing this collection of poems, *Love Is a Dangerous Word*, by Essex Hemphill (1957–1995), a fundamental question we faced was: How might we structure a selected volume offering a distilled and compelling selection of Hemphill's poems, including his best-known poetic works, which appeared in several published volumes during his lifetime, most notably the anthological *Ceremonies: Prose and Poetry* (Plume, 1992) and the chapbooks *Conditions* (Be Bop Books, 1986) and *Earth Life* (Be Bop Books, 1988). For this volume, we have reprinted all of the poems in *Ceremonies,* some of which initially appeared in slight or significant variation in the chapbooks, in order to present the final versions, that Hemphill selected and approved.

The chapbooks, however, also include other poems that did not subsequently appear in *Ceremonies,* and so this volume aims to share many of these poems with readers. *Conditions* is important to consider in this regard, as Hemphill structured it as a continuous suite of poems, each poem titled by a successive roman numeral, creating what might be read as a book-length volume. Hemphill had previously published many of the *Conditions* poems under other titles in literary periodicals, as the "Notes" section at the back of that volume makes clear. Yet when he republished them in *Ceremonies,* he returned in most cases to the original published versions with their journal titles. We have reproduced the *Ceremonies* versions in the order they appear in that volume; for those *Conditions* poems that did not have titles, we chose the opening line, placed in brackets, as the title, in a gesture to the chapbook's original format and style. In at least one case, Hemphill combined several of the *Conditions* poems to produce a new poem for *Ceremonies,* which we have also included. Additionally, we have chosen to include a small sampling of uncollected poems that initially appeared in critic and scholar Dadland Maye's unpublished graduate student project *The Essex Hemphill Reader,* as well as poems that we culled from the rich trove of archival materials in the Essex Hemphill and Wayson Jones collection held at the New York Public Library's Schomburg Center for Research in Black Culture.

The order of the poems in this selected volume mirrors that of Hemphill's published books; we chose to first feature the poems from *Ceremonies,* followed by poems from the chapbooks.

Following these works are the uncollected poems, some unpublished in Hemphill's lifetime, from the start of his career until his untimely passing, in order to give the reader a fuller view of his poetic artistry and range. The earliest of these poems precede the publication of the chapbooks and *Ceremonies*, and the latest follow the anthology by several years. These poems, much like those for which Hemphill received acclaim in his lifetime, offer a window into his formal development, skill, and practice, as well as his interests and concerns, from his dawning sexual and romantic experiences as a Black gay man in the late 1970s and early 1980s, to his individual and collaborative performance work, to his deep engagement with literary and popular culture, to his social and political activism before and during the worst years of the AIDS pandemic, the Reagan-Bush era, the Cold War, the crack epidemic of the 1980s, state violence, and more. Many of the later poems specifically address the challenges and necessities of experiencing desire, sex, and love as a Black queer person, living with HIV/AIDS, as U.S. society shifted ever more into social, political, and economic conservatism and neoliberalism.

Throughout Hemphill's poetry, what we registered was his attentiveness to craft as well as statement, to the possibilities of performance, of form, of the line, and to the expressive content, which is to say the lives and stories, his life and story, that these lines bore and made visible. He was a lyric poet to his core, and a political poet who knew that the most devastating critique could hinge on many of poetry's numerous resources, any of which he wielded when needed. What we also appreciated was how open he was to self-reflection and reassessment, and how much he anticipated and opened up spaces for an array of poetics and poetries to come. I, like so many other writers of my generation and subsequent generations, would not be publishing today if it weren't for Essex Hemphill's example, his courage and daring, and his fearlessness and willingness to place his art on the stage and page before audiences and readers.

Rereading and assembling these poems took on a particular poignancy for me, because I had the pleasure, as a young writer, not only of meeting and interviewing Hemphill in 1989, as part of the Dark Room Writing Collective's reading series, based then in Cambridge, Massachusetts, but of having Hemphill serve as one of my first editors, when he selected and then proceeded to help me refine one of my first published short stories for the anthology

Brother to Brother. He was generous but rigorous in his comments, never failing to suggest striking or rewriting passages that I was wedded to, a process which, I realized on rereading, showed me the breadth of his talents as a reader and writer. Co-editing this collection of poems, I would not deign to change a word, but in studying Hemphill's poetics, how he drafted, ordered, and revised his poems, I continue to learn invaluable lessons about poetic craft and literary art in general. I also believe his generosity of spirit and intellectual and artistic rigor shine through in these selected poems.

Reading Hemphill's work reminds me not only of his remarkable individual talent and many gifts as a poet, but also that he was one of the leading and most accomplished figures in a generation of Black gay, lesbian, transgender, and queer writers and artists who came of age in the wake of the Civil Rights, Black Arts, Gay Liberation and LGBTQ Equality, Women's Rights, Lesbian Separatist, and Black and Third World Feminism movements. His work, like that of his peers, powerfully reflected, acknowledged, assimilated, and advanced the best lessons of these movements. Like a number of his Black LGBTQ peers, Hemphill began publishing and performing his work as more spaces—journals, little magazines, anthologies, and small presses, many edited and published by Black LGBTQ writers and artists, along with reading and screening venues, including bookstores, colleges and universities, conferences, and nightclubs, etc.—opened up and welcomed these artists' visions and voices. For a moment, a flowering of Black LGBTQ literary and artistic production was visible to anyone paying attention. Hemphill even started his own small press, Be Bop Books, in Washington, D.C. I am also reminded that within a few years, the AIDS pandemic took so many of these talented writers from us, often abruptly and before many could realize the rich promise of the work they had shared with the world; and so this selected volume stands as a tribute to Hemphill's distinctive poetics, but also should send us back to those many poets, writers, artists, whom we lost prematurely to AIDS and other social, political, and economic depredations, especially as we witness yet more waves of anti-LGBTQ, racist, misogynistic, and classist backlash to the achievements these movements have made.

In conclusion, co-editing this volume was a labor of deep love and gratitude and tribute. It is our sincere hope that readers will return to it regularly and seek out more of Essex Hemphill's work and that of his LGBTQ contemporaries, who created vital and enduring artistic and activist spaces—fusing the two in ways we might take for granted today—for those who would come after them, making possible the ever-expanding universe of letters in American, African American, and African Diasporic LGBTQ writing that we appreciate today. In addition to my coeditor Robert F. Reid-Pharr, I want to offer my deepest thanks to the late Essex Hemphill, the Hemphill family, Brittany Dennison, Declan Spring, New Directions, agent Jade Wong-Baxter, Dadland Maye, Yaoquan Chen, Reginald Harris, Steven G. Fullwood (special thanks!), the New York Public Library's Schomburg Center for Research in Black Culture, and all the other supporters of this effort to bring Essex Hemphill's work to readers.

New Directions Paperbooks—a partial listing

Adonis, Songs of Mihyar the Damascene
César Aira, Ghosts
  An Episode in the Life of a Landscape Painter
Ryunosuke Akutagawa, Kappa
Will Alexander, Refractive Africa
Osama Alomar, The Teeth of the Comb
Guillaume Apollinaire, Selected Writings
Jessica Au, Cold Enough for Snow
Paul Auster, The Red Notebook
Ingeborg Bachmann, Malina
Honoré de Balzac, Colonel Chabert
Djuna Barnes, Nightwood
Charles Baudelaire, The Flowers of Evil*
Bei Dao, City Gate, Open Up
Yevgenia Belorusets, Lucky Breaks
Rafael Bernal, His Name Was Death
Mei-Mei Berssenbrugge, Empathy
Max Blecher, Adventures in Immediate Irreality
Jorge Luis Borges, Labyrinths
  Seven Nights
Coral Bracho, Firefly Under the Tongue*
Kamau Brathwaite, Ancestors
Anne Carson, Glass, Irony & God
  Wrong Norma
Horacio Castellanos Moya, Senselessness
Camilo José Cela, Mazurka for Two Dead Men
Louis-Ferdinand Céline
  Death on the Installment Plan
  Journey to the End of the Night
Inger Christensen, alphabet
Julio Cortázar, Cronopios and Famas
Jonathan Creasy (ed.), Black Mountain Poems
Robert Creeley, If I Were Writing This
H.D., Selected Poems
Guy Davenport, 7 Greeks
Amparo Dávila, The Houseguest
Osamu Dazai, The Flowers of Buffoonery
  No Longer Human
  The Setting Sun
Anne de Marcken
  It Lasts Forever and Then It's Over
Helen DeWitt, The Last Samurai
  Some Trick
José Donoso, The Obscene Bird of Night
Robert Duncan, Selected Poems
Eça de Queirós, The Maias
Juan Emar, Yesterday

William Empson, 7 Types of Ambiguity
Mathias Énard, Compass
Shusaku Endo, Deep River
Jenny Erpenbeck, Go, Went, Gone
  Kairos
Lawrence Ferlinghetti
  A Coney Island of the Mind
Thalia Field, Personhood
F. Scott Fitzgerald, The Crack-Up
Rivka Galchen, Little Labors
Forrest Gander, Be With
Romain Gary, The Kites
Natalia Ginzburg, The Dry Heart
Henry Green, Concluding
Marlen Haushofer, The Wall
Victor Heringer, The Love of Singular Men
Felisberto Hernández, Piano Stories
Hermann Hesse, Siddhartha
Takashi Hiraide, The Guest Cat
Yoel Hoffmann, Moods
Susan Howe, My Emily Dickinson
  Concordance
Bohumil Hrabal, I Served the King of England
Qurratulain Hyder, River of Fire
Sonallah Ibrahim, That Smell
Rachel Ingalls, Mrs. Caliban
Christopher Isherwood, The Berlin Stories
Fleur Jaeggy, Sweet Days of Discipline
Alfred Jarry, Ubu Roi
B.S. Johnson, House Mother Normal
James Joyce, Stephen Hero
Franz Kafka, Amerika: The Man Who Disappeared
Yasunari Kawabata, Dandelions
Mieko Kanai, Mild Vertigo
John Keene, Counternarratives
Kim Hyesoon, Autobiography of Death
Heinrich von Kleist, Michael Kohlhaas
Taeko Kono, Toddler-Hunting
László Krasznahorkai, Satantango
  Seiobo There Below
Ágota Kristóf, The Illiterate
Eka Kurniawan, Beauty Is a Wound
Mme. de Lafayette, The Princess of Clèves
Lautréamont, Maldoror
Siegfried Lenz, The German Lesson
Alexander Lernet-Holenia, Count Luna

*BILINGUAL EDITION

For a complete listing, request a free catalog from New Directions, 80 8th Avenue, New York, NY 10011
or visit us online at ndbooks.com